the
STUDENT FINANCE GUIDE

FEES, GRANTS AND WHAT IT COSTS

SEAN COUGHLAN

Customer led, ethically guided

**KOGAN
PAGE**

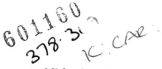

Publisher's note

Every possible effort has been made to ensure that the information contained in this book is accurate at the time of going to press, and the publishers and authors cannot accept responsibility for any errors or omissions, however caused. No responsibility for loss or damage occasioned to any person acting, or refraining from action, as a result of the material in this publication can be accepted by the editor, the publisher or any of the authors.

This guide is published in association with UCAS. UCAS is the organization responsible for managing applications to higher education courses in England, Scotland, Wales and Northern Ireland. Its commercial subsidiary is involved in publishing, event management and the marketing of data and media.

First published in Great Britain in 2005

Kogan Page Limited
120 Pentonville Road
London N1 9JN
United Kingdom
www.kogan-page.co.uk

British Library Cataloguing in Publication Data

A CIP record for this book is available from the British Library.

ISBN 0 7494 4428 2

Typeset by Jean Cussons Typesetting, Diss, Norfolk
Printed and bound in Great Britain by Cambridge University Press

ifs level 3 Certificate in Financial Studies (CeFS)

ifs level 3 Diploma in Financial Studies (Dip FS)

Finances are a necessary part of our lives at whatever stage we are at and the Institute of Financial Services (**ifs**) believes it is an essential part of education too.

Savings
Investments
Expenses
Phones
Adventure
Clothes

Are you ready?

Parties
Bills
Tax
Food
Mortgages
Rent
Pensions

 institute of financial services
School of Finance

Further information

For further information about CeFS or Dip FS simply contact the **ifs** on 01227 828259 or email dbuck@ifslearning.com

The Institute of Financial Services (*ifs*) is a leading provider of financial education

As a school of finance, we provide for the formal learning needs of consumers and those employed within the industry, both in the UK and in key markets worldwide.

Our qualifications for consumers seek to equip people with the essential life skills of personal financial management. *ifs* qualifications are taught in schools and colleges throughout the UK and offer a meaningful solution to the problems of poor financial literacy. Our comprehensive provision for financial literacy now also includes *ifs*ProShare, which offers student investor competitions and employee share ownership initiatives.

For those employed in the industry, our qualifications and ongoing learning programmes aim to recognize and raise standards of professionalism.

ifs qualifications range from certificates for regulated sales activities, such as the giving of investment and mortgage advice, through to specialist Diplomas in financial services management, and the flagship BSC (Hons) in Financial Services and Associateship offered in partnership with the University of Manchester.

Contents

Whatever your plans for the future, it pays to do your homework.

School Leaver Opportunities

Whether you're intending to go to university or are still undecided about your future, PricewaterhouseCoopers can give your career a real kick-start.

You see, although you may think we only look for graduates who've studied a business or finance related degree, we're actually interested in people from all walks of life. In fact, the only thing that can match the diversity of our people, is the diversity of opportunities we can offer school leavers.

From our Open Days and Gap Year Placements to our Flying Start degree programme, we have something for everyone. And you can rest assured, whichever programme catches your eye, you'll gain a real insight into how a professional services firm operates and develop skills you'll use throughout your future career.

To find out more, visit our website, or call us on freephone 0808 100 1500.

www.pwc.com/uk/careers/

PricewaterhouseCoopers (PwC) is one of the world's largest professional services organisations and our 120,000 people around the globe help organisations - businesses, charities and even governments – measure their financial performance and improve the way they work. This could involve conducting audits of their company results, giving them tax advice, or pointers on how to manage their risks more effectively. We work with a wide variety of clients, so you could find yourself working with a Premiership football club, a top fashion house or even a music TV channel. And, because of the variety of work we do, we're always looking for talented young people to join our firm each year through our school leaver, undergraduate and graduate opportunities.

The PwC Gap Year Programme is perfect for students who are planning on taking a year out before university. During the seven-month placement, students are given real work and real responsibilities – a great way to develop business and interpersonal skills for the future. Students who impress us during their placement are rewarded with a Scholarship of £1,500 each year at university and paid work experience during vacations. It really is the beginning of a long-term relationship, as you could find yourself joining as a graduate a few years down the line.

PwC have also joined forces with the University of Newcastle and the Institute of Chartered Accountants in England and Wales (ICAEW) to offer a unique Business Accounting and Finance degree offering successful students an accelerated route to becoming a qualified Chartered Accountant. Paid work placements with PwC and a specially designed exam syllabus ensure that you get a head start in your Accountancy career.

If you would like to find out more about PwC and the career opportunities on offer, why not visit our careers website **www.pwc.com/uk/careers/** or contact our Student Helpline on **0808 100 1500**.

people:skills:jobs:

Department for
**Employment
and Learning**
www.delni.gov.uk

The Future of Higher Education in Northern Ireland

Tuition Fees and Student Finance arrangements from September 2006

Tuition Fees

Higher education providers will be able to charge fees of up to £3,000 to new full time undergraduate students.

Deferred Fees

Full time undergraduate students will not have to pay up front tuition fees before or during their higher education courses. They will be able to defer payment through a fee loan.

Grants and Maintenance Loans

New full time students from lower income households will be eligible for a means tested maintenance grant of up to £3,200 and a maintenance loan to meet their basic living costs.

Supplementary grants for students with children, and students with disabilities will continue as at present.

NB Existing students, who started before September 2006, will continue to be subject to the current fee of approx £1,200 (which may also be deferred through a fee loan) and to be eligible for the higher education bursary of up to £2,000 per year.

FOR MORE INFORMATION PLEASE CONTACT OUR WEBSITE: **www.delni.gov.uk/studentfinance**

advertisement feature

Setting the Standard

AQA is an educational charity which offers high quality examinations. We are the largest A Level board - issuing some 750,000 AS and A Level results each summer - and are also providers of GCSE, GNVQ, VCE and Entry Level.

Our priority is accurate assessment for all our candidates and we work closely with teachers in schools and colleges to achieve it. AQA offers an unparalleled level of guidance to teachers with an annual schedule of 1500 support meetings which are attended by a total of 50,000 teachers.

AQA has an extensive research programme. We are in the forefront of improving the quality of service to students, schools and colleges with the introduction of new technology including on-screen assessment and electronic marking.

For further information about AQA please visit our Website.

www.aqa.org.uk

Wesser and Partner are the pioneer of face to face fundraising. Starting in Germany in 1968 and launching in the UK in 1997, we have over 35 years of fundraising experience. We have raised over 4 million supporters for worthy charities across Europe and over 10,000 young people have worked with us.

Wesser and Partner work solely on behalf of St. John Ambulance in the UK, providing them with a professional fundraising campaign that ensures they have vital funds to carry on the exceptional work that they do. The work that St John does affects one in five people at some point in their lifetime; their motto is 'Caring for Life', and supporting such a worthwhile charity is a great experience.

Working for us and supporting St John can be some of the most rewarding work students can do with their time during their Easter, Summer or Christmas breaks. Fundraisers have a genuine opportunity to know that they are contributing to the community with their time and hard work.

Naturally, however, no one works for free! And Wesser and Partner know how to recognize people who work hard and are committed to excellence, regardless of their age, education or background. We pride ourselves on offering unbelievable opportunities to students, such as the potential for promotion in just 6 weeks! Through ongoing training we can give people vital skills in Sales and Marketing as well as helping them to improve their administration and communication.

We pay a great basic, plus loads of incentives and bonuses, both for the individual and the team. The average fundraiser earns £1200+ a month!

The typical day in the life of a fundraiser is challenging and varied with most of the work taking place in the afternoon and evenings. Fundraisers work with like-minded people in teams of between 4 and 8, which means that there's no chance of anything getting boring! Wesser and Partner also provide free accommodation for all our teams, plus a car for their use!

Everything is paid for except food and petrol. The perfect job for students wanting to make lots of money during their holidays!

We do not require any previous experience or qualifications, we simply look for people who are confident, outgoing, and most importantly, hard working!

student finance wales

invest in your future

The provision of student funding in England and Wales is going to be changing soon.

From 2006/07 the National Assembly for Wales will have the power to decide what levels of tuition fees and student support will apply in Wales.

The important information for students living in Wales can be seen at:

www.studentfinancewales.co.uk

buddsodda yn dy ddyfodol

cyllid myfyrwyr cymru

Mae'r drefn o ddarparu cyllid i fyfyrwyr yng Nghymru a Lloegr ar fin newid.

O 2006/07 ymlaen bydd gan Gynulliad Cenedlaethol Cymru y pwer i benderfynu pa lefel o ffioedd dysgu a chymorth i fyfyrwyr a fydd yn gymwys i Gymru.

Gellir gweld y wybodaeth bwysig i fyfyrwyr sy'n byw yng Nghymru ar wefan Cyllid Myfyrwyr Cymru:

www.cyllidmyfyrwyrcymru.co.uk

Foreword: The UCAS Guide to Student Finance

Preparing for your future can be a daunting but exciting task. Many factors should be considered when planning your application to higher education, such as where and what you would like to study, and which career you would like to pursue after completing the course. Concerns about expenses, however, can have an impact upon your decisions. Although the current changes to student funding may sometimes appear to be a little confusing, there is much advice available which will help you keep up to date with the opportunities and assistance available to you. Attending a university or college may be the first time you will be managing your money for yourself; planning the way you spend and save is essential, and researching your options can help you plan your time and finances effectively.

Learning to budget as a student is a skill that will benefit you throughout your life. Whether you have to pay tuition fees during or after your course, you will need to consider other expenses. Accommodation, travel and general living costs vary, but you should be able to find the right place at an affordable price. If you have financial difficulties, there are various sources of additional funding, from grants and loans to part-time jobs, which can help you get back on track. Many types of paid employment are available, depending on where you study. Universities and colleges usually have vacancy listings on-site for the local area, or you may find a job at the institution itself – every higher education institution has a students' union which employs both undergraduates and postgraduates, so you could earn money whilst becoming involved in the current issues that affect your student life.

Depending on the course you study and your personal circumstances, you may be eligible for one of the scholarships or bursaries available: details can be found at www.ucas.com and the Office for Fair Access website www.offa.org.uk. Information about student loans is available from the Student Loans Company Limited, www.slc.co.uk. If you are currently attending a school or college, you can apply for a UCAS card: this card offers discounts for various products, which could help you save money. You may also wish to open a student bank account as a vehicle for managing your money more effectively.

The advantages of being a graduate put any financial concerns into perspective. Along with broadening your intellect, developing social skills and gaining independence, obtaining a higher education qualification improves career prospects available to you and subsequently can enhance your long-term financial success. The cost of applying to higher education is an issue that must be considered and planned for but it is an investment in your future that should reap great benefits.

On behalf of UCAS, may I wish you every success for the future.

Anthony McClaran
Chief Executive, UCAS

Introduction

Going to university or college is a big decision. In fact, it's lots of big decisions. Which course will you choose? To which institutions are you going to apply? Where will you live if you accept the offer of a place?

But here's a question that's not going to be easy to ignore. How much will it cost to get a degree? And, for that matter, how much will it cost if you don't go into higher education?

There are all kinds of ways of looking at the decision to go to university or college – from the funsville social life to the joys of academic endeavour to the prospect of getting a well-paid job afterwards. But putting all these important considerations aside, students, and their anxious parents, will be looking back to the gritty financial question. How much money does it cost to go into higher education?

It's a straightforward question. But don't expect a straightforward answer, because student finance is confusing. There's no point trying to avoid what is plainly the case, especially when it's about to get even more complicated, with another major overhaul in autumn 2006.

Student funding has been in upheaval for at least the last two decades, and each change has added more layers of detail, with different systems often running concurrently, as different year groups operate under different funding arrangements.

Tuition fees, grants, student loans, bursaries, parental contributions and graduate repayments all get shouted about as if everyone knew what they meant and, more to the point, how much money was involved. It's like a blizzard of confusing terms. Tuition fees? Are they the same as top-up fees? And what are variable fees? In fact, they're all about the same fees, but how much they'll cost is another question entirely.

This book is an attempt to hack a path through the student finance jungle, in a way that doesn't turn it into some kind of exercise in incomprehensible accountancy. It is complicated, but once you get an overview of how the system works, you should then be able to get into the detail of how much it will cost in your particular circumstances.

Because the answer to the 'how much will it cost?' question will be different for every student. Much of student support is means-tested, so the amount each student receives and will have to pay will vary depending on his or her family's income. This already probably sounds like it's getting into the too-much-detail area, but if you are considering going to university or college this book should allow you to get a grasp on how you will be charged and the help that should be available to you.

The book begins by looking at some of the big questions about university finance. Is it worth it? Will parents be able to afford it? And then it lays out the two sides of the equation: 'Financial support for students' and 'How much will it cost?'

So, on one side of the balance sheet, you have all the expenditure facing students and their parents, such as fees and accommodation. And on the other side are the types of support available to help students cover their costs, in the form of grants, subsidies and loans.

Although there are often headlines screaming about the cost of going to university or college, it's pretty meaningless unless you also look at what's on offer to offset those expenses.

This double-headed approach means some repetition, and I don't make any apology for that, because this isn't a simple system to understand, and for anyone dipping into the book, it might give them the information they need without having to plough through the entire book.

The outcome of the balancing act between costs and support can vary greatly between different students. For a student whose family is on a very low income, the costs of going on to higher education will be considerably lower than for students from a rich family.

Students from middle-income families – probably the majority –

will be looking more closely at the small print to see to what extent they will qualify for support or whether they will be squeezed out.

And just to add to the mix, the shake-up of the tuition fees system in autumn 2006 will mean further costs and higher levels of support in compensation. Most significantly, it will take away the requirement to pay fees in advance. Instead they'll be repaid when students have graduated and are working.

But higher fees will mean higher debts, and for students weighing up their higher education options it will mean a decision with higher stakes. And as an increasing proportion of young people go to university or college, then opting out of getting a degree will have its own consequences for career prospects.

So for anyone considering that great leap forward into university or college, good luck, and hopefully this book will help to soften the landing.

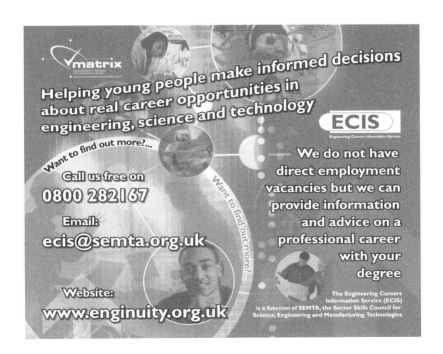

The Engineering Careers Information Service was established in 1976 and is an information and advisory service for young people and those who advise them. Most enquiries are dealt with through a free phone service or e-mail. (See attached advert.)

A career with an engineering degree can offer some real opportunities that can vary significantly. Employment is just as likely in a career with a company in the food and drink or clothing sectors as in a traditional engineering sub sector such as aerospace.

Engineering is all around us literally. Good graduate engineers will need to have good team working skills as most professional engineers work as a member of a group, each offering their particular skill and expertise to solve problems and not least deliver a project on time. Do some research? What sort of employment prospects fit your degree? Are there any trends, e.g. growing or declining employment levels?

If you are able consider a gap year in a role that will build on your degree studies, – perhaps a job in industry on route to graduation – go for it! The experience will provide you with a practical reflection on your academic studies and enhance your employability following graduation. Yes you will take an extra year to graduate but you could well have reduced your debts and loans as a result.

Real professional engineers will have letters after their name, I.Eng. or C.Eng. as an Incorporated or Chartered Engineer respectively. They will be registered via a professional engineering institution with the Engineering Council UK. Do consider pursuing this status after graduation with an agreed programme of professional development.

It is also worth mentioning that a growing number of professional engineers are employed by international companies. You could easily find yourself working for an employer based overseas. Foreign travel is a real option that you might find attractive. If you enjoy speaking a modern foreign language, this could be a great asset to you as an engineer. Unfortunately to few Brits have the ability to converse in a second language!

Finally remember that engineering graduates have many employment opportunities available to them because of their so-called 'transferable skills'. So you will be of interest to employers outside engineering as well as within it. It tends not to work the other way round for non-engineering/technical graduates.

Do ask us about Insight, a university one-week taster course for females only in lower sixth form pursuing maths and science at AS level/Scottish Highers.

Good luck with your learning studies.

John Bristow
Careers & Education Manager
SEMTA

Part One

University challenge

An ethical approach to banking

Surprisingly perhaps, only one UK high street bank works to a strict Ethical Policy – and that is The Co-operative Bank.

The Co-operative Bank's Ethical Policy was introduced back in 1992 to set out precisely the ethical standards which would govern the types of businesses to which the bank would - and would not - offer services. It set these ethical standards by asking its customers which issues concerned them. After all, it is generally their money that is invested in businesses – and so they should have a say in how it is used.

Back in 1992, more than 80% of the Bank's customers thought that it was a good idea to have an Ethical Policy. This support has since increased to 97%. Each year, up to 30% or so of the businesses which apply to open an account with the bank are rejected because they do not meet the Bank's ethical standards. At the same time, however, the Bank seeks to support organisations which share the Bank's approach to society and the environment.

When you take out a loan from The Co-operative Bank, you can be certain that the money you borrow has not come from the profits of any activities which conflict with the policy. These cover such issues as:

- Human Rights
- The Arms Trade
- Corporate Responsibility and Global Trade
- Genetic Modification
- Social Enterprise
- Ecological Impact
- Animal Welfare

To find out more about The Co-operative Bank's Ethical Policy, phone **08457 212 212**, call into your local branch or visit **www.co-operativebank.co.uk**

1

Everything in five minutes

If you're in a hurry and just want to see the headlines for student finance, here's a whistle-stop tour of the big questions – showing the type of expenses facing students and their families and the support that is available.

Tuition fees

Students starting in autumn 2005 will have to pay an up-front tuition fee, up to a maximum of £1,175. This is the last intake of students to use this system. From 2006, in English universities, tuition fees will be up to £3,000 per year, but will be paid back in instalments after students have graduated and are working.

Grants

Along with higher fees, there will be a new type of grant in 2006, worth up to £2,700, which will be targeted at lower-income families. How the income thresholds will be applied is not yet known. As a warm-up act, there is a smaller grant in 2005, worth up to £1,000, for low-income families.

Universities are also planning to introduce bursaries to help poorer students, many of which will be worth £3,000 per year.

Student loans

You can also borrow a student loan to cover living costs, such as rent, of up to a maximum of £4,195 per year for students at universities or colleges outside London, £5,175 in London and £3,320 for those living at home.

Parents will pay...

The first 75 per cent of the loan is available to all students, regardless of parental income. The next 25 per cent is means-tested – the richer the parents, the lower the loan. The means-tested loan that these 'richer' students don't get is to be replaced by the 'parental contribution'.

The maximum that a parent of a student outside London will have to pay is £2,225 per year, which constitutes the tuition fee and a parental contribution towards living costs. To have to pay this amount, the combined income of parents will be above £42,720.

If the combined income of parents is not more than £32,744, they will have to contribute towards tuition fees, but not towards the student's living costs – for which the full student loan will be available.

If the household income is below £20,010, then parents will not have to pay anything towards either the tuition fee or living costs.

Living costs

The loan is meant to cover living costs such as rent and bills. These costs vary depending on the location and lifestyle of a student, but don't be surprised if this adds up to about £7,000 per year. This amount is higher than the maximum student loan available, which means that you will either have to depend on part-time jobs or further borrowing. Often students depend on both.

Part-time jobs

No longer an occasional sideline, part-time jobs are now a mainstream requirement for many students. The increase in term-time jobs has been one of the major changes in the student lifestyle in the last few years. About two in five students now have regular part-time jobs during term-time, earning an average of £86 per week.

Student debt

Students take part-time jobs to get spending money and to avoid borrowing. But the amount owed by students continues to climb. A survey from Barclays showed that the average graduate debt had increased by more than 500 per cent in the decade after 1994. Surveys suggest average debt now stands at around £10,000 to £13,000. But it should be remembered that the largest part of this will be debts owed to the Student Loans Company, which are interest free and only paid back when a student is in a regular job.

Good investment?

This is the crunch question. If you pay for a higher education course, will there be a return on your money? The latest evidence suggests that graduates are still way ahead in the income stakes, although the gap with non-graduates is closing. At present, graduates earn on average 41 per cent more per hour than non-graduates. Previous international surveys have claimed that the difference is 59 per cent. Even with the lower figure, the cost of university or college would quickly be recovered by the salary advantage. Having a degree remains the key to many high-status jobs. In 'professional' occupations, the overwhelming majority of people will have been to university or college.

England, Scotland, Wales and Northern Ireland

The higher education systems in the United Kingdom are becoming increasingly different. The changes to tuition fees in 2006 in England will make them even more different. Although Northern Ireland, for the moment, looks set to follow the English changes, they will not be implemented in Scotland or Wales. In Scotland students do not pay tuition fees and there is a separate system of repayment and grants.

2

Is it worth it?

The good old days

If you went to university or college in the old days student finance was a simple enough question. You got a grant at the beginning of term. Once you spent it, probably on a purple corduroy suit or a particularly challenging concept album, you didn't have any more money, because no one else would give you any. You'd blown it, so tough. You'd get another grant next term.

There were no tuition fees, no student loans, no repayments and no student debts unless you had an indulgent bank manager who'd let you run up an overdraft, maybe for alarmingly high amounts such as £20 or £30. Books on student finance wouldn't have got past a couple of paragraphs. And there wouldn't have been much of a readership either, because only a small proportion of young people went on to higher education.

Funding today and in the future

All this has changed. In the next few years, young people going to university or college will probably be in the majority rather than a small minority. And the way that they are funded through higher education will also be completely different from the system familiar to the parents of today's would-be students.

It's now part of the equation that students have to make an individual contribution towards the cost of going to university or college, on the basis that they will individually benefit from getting a degree. And from 2006, this contribution is going to include up to £3,000 a year in tuition fees.

And to get round to the key question: is it worth it?

In the days before fees and loans, it was a no-brainer. At no personal outlay, you were being given three years of higher education leading to a degree that would push up your earnings. Of course it was worth it. Even if at the end of three years you went to live in a commune in Peru, you'd still come back as a graduate, with a head start in the careers race.

The only cost to be factored in, apart from any modest parental contributions to the maintenance grant, was the loss of earnings for three years. But, objectively, the benefits were clearly greater than the debits. So, unsurprisingly, better-off families were enthusiastic users of a higher education system that offered such generous subsidies for a relatively small number of young people.

But now the talk is of 'mass participation' and 'widening access' to higher education, which also translates as 'mass payment' and 'widening the wallet' because everyone now has to pay something towards covering the cost.

The tuition fee, in place for the past seven years, is currently £1,175 and will rise in 2006 to £3,000 per year. Student loans, which have to be repaid, can be up to £5,175 per year. And, on Planet Reality, students are likely to run up other debts on credit cards and bank overdrafts.

Typical estimates for how much students now owe when they leave higher education are between £10,000 and £12,000. And researchers have calculated that the hike in fees will add another 50 per cent to this, pushing up average graduate debt towards £15,000 to £18,000.

There have been far higher estimates, including from banks, which say that under the new system graduate debt is more likely to be in the region of £30,000.

Will I get a return on the investment?

With these kind of costs attached to going to university or college, is it worth it? Setting aside the philosophical debates about the inherent value of education, and focusing on the cash, there are two key ways of getting to the answer.

First, is it value for money, and does the price reflect the value? Higher education institutions will shout deafeningly that the cost paid by students is nowhere near the real cost of their higher education. There is still a substantial subsidy built into the pricing system.

Universities and colleges, for as long as anyone can remember, have always been broke and saying they need the kind of big bucks available to the most prestigious universities in the United States. And part of their complaint is that providing tuition, premises, equipment and assessment for undergraduates is very expensive.

Many universities also say that the £3,000 per year upper limit for tuition fees is disastrously low and will continue lobbying for an increase, which they say is necessary to pay for the cost of teaching this ever-increasing number of students.

So how much of a bargain are students getting? This varies between universities and courses, but the government says that, on average, the current £1,175 fee represents a quarter of the real cost of a university or college place.

Students will say that they have to pay for their living costs as well as tuition fees. But universities and colleges would argue that that's not really their problem – and that if these young people were working, they'd still have living costs to pay.

The second question to ask is whether going to university or college really pays off as an investment. You might be getting a bargain in terms of higher education costs, but can you usefully apply the degree? This is an important debate – and there isn't an undisputed answer.

Salary prospects

According to an international survey from the Organisation for Economic Co-operation and Development (OECD) people with degrees in the UK earn on average 59 per cent more than those without degrees. This represents a major financial advantage for graduates – it is one of the biggest gaps between graduates and non-graduates in the industrialized world.

It means that a debt of £15,000 will rapidly be outweighed by higher earnings. And the government has calculated that the average graduate will earn an extra £400,000 over the course of their working lives. Such huge figures are designed to make a political point – showing that the new fees system shouldn't deter university and college applicants. But there is undoubtedly an underlying truth that the jobs market is heavily biased towards people with degrees.

There are numerous exceptions to this, whether it's Richard Branson or John Major, showing you don't need a degree to succeed. But, on average, graduates have long dominated the upper-income jobs. There's plenty of anecdotal stuff about how much plumbers and builders are earning. But the reality is that the quids-in crowd are the professionals with degrees.

Any serious survey of the labour market shows that graduates are at a considerable advantage. Businesses might complain that they want more high-skilled workers, rather than media studies students, but, when there is such a heavy income premium in favour of graduates, they shouldn't be surprised that so many people opt for higher education.

What is now being questioned is whether this advantage will be maintained as the numbers of graduates increase. Put simply, if half the population has a degree, will there be graduate jobs for half the population?

If not, the sceptics would say, students are going to pay for a university or college degree and end up working in A level jobs. This view argues that as the supply of graduates increases the financial advantage of having a degree will decline.

A widely reported graduate careers survey in 2004 showed that only a third of graduates were going straight into graduate jobs – the lowest level for a decade – prompting speculation that too many graduates were flooding the jobs market. Against such an interpretation you can argue that many graduates take time before settling into a career. Even if the advantage declines by half, it will still mean that graduates can command a seriously better income than non-graduates.

And, more to the point, it raises questions about what will happen to those non-graduates, who will be pushed even further back in the queue for the best jobs. Just as going to university or college has financial implications, so too does choosing not to go. The salary advantage to graduates represents a pretty tough penalty to those who are non-graduates.

But what are the prospects for students who are leaving university or college now? Are there enough graduate jobs for graduates?

Figures released in 2005 by the Association of Graduate Recruiters showed an extremely buoyant jobs market for new graduates, with typical starting salaries up 4.8 per cent, the highest rise for five years. The 'median' graduate starting salary is £22,000, with promises of 'significant increases in vacancies'. This regular survey of employers found a continuing strong demand for graduates, with a 14.5 per cent annual increase in 'graduate positions', following a 15.5 per cent increase last year.

The rate of salary increase is also likely to be stronger for graduates. A London university tracking the progress of its graduates found that a fifth were earning more than £40,000 within three years of leaving university.

So far the experience in countries with high numbers of graduates has been that there has not been a reduction in the financial advantages. And it has been claimed that increasing the proportion of graduates in itself stimulates the creation of more jobs.

The most detailed research on the financial returns from getting a degree in the UK gives some support for both the sceptics and the optimists about expanding numbers in higher education. Published in February 2005, a government survey shows that graduates are earning much more money than non-graduates, but that the gap is narrowing.

In terms of money earned per hour, a graduate earns on average 43 per cent more than someone with A levels. Four years ago, the earnings gap was 51 per cent. Even if this gap narrows further, it still represents a huge differential in how much money someone is likely to earn. If you were offered a 43 per cent pay hike overnight for the sake of having a qualification, it would seem like a particularly valuable piece of paper.

And the research shows very precisely that, like stepping stones, each level of qualification, from GCSE to A level to a degree, marks a higher level of earnings. It also answers the 'you'd be better off getting a trade' argument. The survey shows that the person who has been through a trade apprenticeship earns, on average, slightly less than someone with A levels, and 47 per cent less than a graduate.

But somehow that still doesn't explain how the plumber can charge me £75 per hour to not fix the boiler.

Putting that aside, for the individual student it means that, at least at present, the returns on going to university or college are very favourable. The survey shows that the average student going on to university or college will be collecting a salary of £28,600 rather than £20,000 if they'd left after A levels. And after a couple of years that difference is going to exceed the student debt.

Parental income

Of course there's no such thing as an 'average' student, particularly when financial support for students varies depending on the income of their parents.

Much attention has been paid to students from poorer backgrounds who might be deterred from going into higher education by the threat of high costs and large debts. But, in practice, students from low-income backgrounds have the least to lose in the funding stakes. Tuition fees will either be paid for them or else, under the new system, students will receive grants equivalent to the cost. And higher education institutions are lining up bursaries to help with living costs for students from low-income families.

If there is a cultural resistance to going to university, then that's a different matter. Because, in terms of pounds and pence, low-income students are going to get most of the breaks under the new funding arrangements, and because of the extra non-repayable grants, they should be able to graduate with smaller debts than other students.

It's a more troubling calculation for students from middle-income families. A couple of parents working in a job like teaching are going to get very little support for their student children, other than the loan available to all students.

The change in the fees system in 2006, which will mean the student repays their own fees when they graduate, will soften the cost to parents, who will no longer have to pay towards up-front fees. But even with that sugar on the pill, middle-income parents, who would not consider themselves even slightly rich, will still be contributing towards their children's living costs, often beyond the £1,300 or so specified by the means-testing.

What has to be decided is whether this short-term sacrifice will lead to sufficient long-term benefits

For the parent, it can be tough. And talk to anyone with more than one student in higher education and they will make that point forcefully. But it's a relatively short-lived financial strain – and cheaper than a new car or an up-market summer holiday. Not that that will be much consolation to parents who got their own higher education without having to pay anything.

This isn't an easy choice. And many middle-income parents will feel that it's not really a choice at all. They don't want their children to miss out on the university or college education that they had themselves – not least because they know how much not having a degree could cost them in the long run.

For the student it's a different type of calculation. The biggest 'Is it worth it?' question concerns the size of the debt they will build up while they're at university or college. And, again, this has to be put into the context of the potential gain in earnings.

It's also important to say that the student loan debt, while being real cash, is not like a commercial loan. It's an interest-free advance, which is only repaid once a student earns the equivalent of £15,000 per year. For a graduate earning £30,000 per year, the repayment on the loan is going to be about £112 per month. But if having a degree provides a 43 per cent boost to earnings then the financial advantage, about £1,000 per month, is going to greatly outweigh the repayment.

Such arbitrary examples are not going to be representative comparisons for everyone. But they suggest how you can approach this question of value for money.

And there are other questions to ask yourself. What are the long-term prospects of promotion within a career for graduates and non-graduates? How much debt might you run up in a low-paying job?

These aren't idle questions. At present the numbers of graduates in the workforce remain fairly low, standing at about a quarter. But, as the expansion in student numbers feeds into the workforce, it's going to mean tougher competition for better-paid jobs. And when half the workforce is made up of graduates, where will that leave the job chances for people who dropped out after their A levels? It's already tight at the top, with almost 82 per cent of people in 'professional' occupations holding a degree.

There are also other difficult-to-quantify aspects to this choice. Going to university or college means being exposed to ideas and experiences which are going to help in working life and beyond. Employers say that life skills, such as being self-organized and having lived away from home, can be as valuable to a graduate as their qualifications.

Students themselves seem to be confident of the value of the investment

The Unite/Mori survey of student attitudes in January 2005 showed that an overwhelming 89 per cent of students either agreed or strongly agreed with the proposition that 'the money I am spending on my education is a good investment in my future'.

But, as they say at the fairground, you pays your money and you takes your choice.

3

Tuition fees: 2006 and all that

When people talk about student finance, tuition fees are often the first item on the agenda. They've been politically controversial, the cause of student protest and confusion among parents.

But the oddest fact about tuition fees (also known as top-up fees) is that, despite their symbolic importance, in terms of hard cash they've never been anything like the most expensive part of going to university or college. At present, the maximum is about £40 per week (on a 30-week academic year). And the average amount actually paid, after subsidies have been taken into account, is just over £19 per week.

Even when fees almost treble in 2006, they are still unlikely to be the majority of a student's debt. Everyday living costs, such as paying the rent and bills, are still going to be more costly, not least because the rent and bills have to be paid with real cash, rather than paid off in instalments over several years.

Tuition fee changes

There are big changes ahead for fees. For students starting in English universities and colleges in autumn 2006 there will be a brand new system of charges. There are a few exceptions to this, such as gap year students who would otherwise have been starting in 2005. But the vast majority of students in 2006 are going to have the pleasure of being guinea pigs for a new set of funding arrangements.

'Deferred Entry' or 'Gap Year' Students Applying through UCAS in 2005 for Entry in 2006

UCAS applicants in receipt of an offer(s) of a deferred entry place for 2006 by 1 August 2005, will qualify for the 'gap year' exemption from variable fees. This means that such applicants will, on entry to their course in 2006, be treated as if they were a September 2005 entrant for fees and other financial support purposes.

The offer can be conditional or unconditional and, although most students are expected to receive their offers through UCAS, the offer can be evidenced through either a UCAS or an institution letter.

If you find yourself without a place after examination results are published you may seek a deferred entry place in Clearing and still qualify for the 'gap year' exemption provided that you can produce evidence that you originally received an offer of a deferred entry place for 2006 by 1 August 2005.

The effect of this is that applicants who receive an offer for deferred entry on or before 1 August 2005 will qualify for the exemption even if they do not actually accept or take up that place. For example an applicant that received an offer or offers (whether conditional or unconditional) and declined those offers or was unsuccessful in obtaining confirmation of the offer(s) following publication of examination results would still qualify for the exemption if gaining a place through Clearing. You will realise that this advice supersedes the statement in the minute of the Review Meeting that 'the entitlement does not transfer to Clearing'.

The Advice Statement states 'the offer can be evidenced through either a UCAS or an institution letter'. This feature may be useful when offering places on 'qualifying' courses that are not covered by the UCAS Applications Recruitment Policy (appendix A of the current UCAS Admissions Guide refers). It also follows that the course undertaken does not necessarily have to be at an institution that recruits through UCAS.

Advice Statement from UCAS

Without going into too much of the political rhetoric, the background to the change has been the demand from higher education institutions for more cash to pay for the increasing numbers of students. Higher education says it is £10 billion short of the cash it needs – and, in response, the government has decided that students should contribute more towards the cost of going to university or college, not least because students will be the ones who stand to benefit from having a degree.

In terms of cash, the extra charge is to be made through the tuition fee – the money paid by a student to the university or college towards the cost of their tuition. This will increase almost three times to a maximum of £3,000 per year. In parallel with this increase, and to prevent students being deterred by the hike in fees, there will also be the reintroduction of non-repayable grants, aimed at poorer students and worth up to £2,700 per year.

These are the twin pillars of the new system: higher fees channelling more money into universities and colleges, and higher support so that poorer students are not disadvantaged.

There is another important change that should benefit all students regardless of their family's income. And that's the way that fees will be paid.

Payment changes

Until 2006, students have had to pay tuition fees at the beginning of the academic year – so-called 'up-front' payments. But, under the new arrangements, fees will not have to be repaid until after the student has graduated and is working. The tuition fee is effectively being wrapped up into an extended student loan.

The student loan system, which provides the funding for a student's living costs such as rent, food and clothes, will continue broadly as before. Students can borrow an interest-free loan from the Student Loans Company to cover these maintenance costs, which will be repaid once the student starts working and earns the equivalent of £15,000 per year.

It's worth getting your head around these basic foundations of the student funding system – and forgive the repetition. Because it's very confusing at the moment when the information available has to explain two different arrangements – the old outgoing system and the new one about to arrive.

But, in a nutshell, if you've been hearing about tuition fees, top-up fees, variable fees or variable deferred fees, all these things are about the £3,000 per year that students will pay to go to university or college from 2006.

Except that the money won't be handed over by the student when he or she starts. It will be paid back in instalments after the student has left higher education and begun a regular job. You won't have to hand over the cash to the university or college, and the only contact with this tuition fee will be repayments taken, like a tax, directly from your monthly salary after graduation.

Students from low-income families will qualify for a government grant and university or college bursaries. And all students will get a student loan from the imaginatively titled Student Loans Company to pay for their living costs – with poorer students entitled to larger loans.

These changes for 2006 have sparked fierce debate across all shades of political opinion. There were accusations that this would put too high a price tag on higher education and that it would end the idea of higher education being a universally available opportunity for all. There were other views, also strongly held, that universities and colleges were starved of funding and it was completely fair to ask those who would benefit from higher education to pay something back, especially when there was financial support to help young people from deprived backgrounds.

Almost since the demise of the old-style maintenance grants, there has been a constant tinkering with the student funding system, adding layer upon layer of complication. Now it seems that the system of fees, grants and loans is being firmly entrenched.

It's also worth flagging up that this direction for student funding in England marks another step towards a devolved education system within the United Kingdom. English universities and colleges will be taking their own route, making it less and less relevant to generalize about funding systems across England, Scotland, Wales and Northern Ireland.

The introduction of these changes in England has been debated furiously, but the impact still remains a matter of speculation, and it will only really become clear once the 2006 admissions process gets under way.

There have been claims that the higher fees will discourage working-class youngsters from applying. But it could also be argued that they will be offered more financial support than ever before and so could be attracted in greater numbers.

There are already elements of the new system that have not fallen into the expected pattern. There was much talk of a 'market' in tuition fees emerging, with universities and colleges setting a variety of different charges for courses. The £3,000 would be the upper limit, but there could be universities and colleges where all the courses would be £1,500 or where individual courses would be somewhere in the range between zero and £3,000.

In fact, almost none of this has happened, and most higher education institutions appear to be planning to charge £3,000 for all their courses. The institutions argue that £3,000 is too low an upper limit and that they can't afford to charge any less.

There are going to be a handful of exceptions to this £3,000 charge – at the time of writing, by eight universities – but it's nothing like the amount of diversity that the government might have expected.

Proving that life is nothing if not surprising, while the tuition fee market has failed to emerge there has been a flowering of a different kind of market – in bursaries.

Bursaries

These non-repayable grants, awarded by individual universities and colleges and funded by the higher tuition fees, are set to become an important part of the finance system – sometimes worth more than the full student loan.

They are targeted at specific groups of students, such as those from low-income families, those living in the higher education institution's local area, or even those with very good A levels. And, so far, there have been announcements offering bursaries of between £1,000 and £5,000 per year.

It's still early days, and the success of such financial incentives remains to be seen, but it could be that the bursary system becomes an important part of the recruitment process. In the United States, the awarding of scholarships to students is part of the process of attracting the best academic and sporting talent. And we could be seeing the arrival of such financial incentives at UK universities and colleges.

For 2006, there is already a university offering a bursary for every student accepted with three grade As at A level, regardless of his or her parents' income. If this pulls in the most talented students, then will 2007 see other institutions making similar or higher offers?

The only complication with bursaries is that they're not a centralized system but are operated independently by each institution, targeting the particular type of students that they want to encourage to apply. So it will be a case of checking out what's on offer from the universities and colleges you're considering.

Because the most likely target for bursaries will be students from low-income families it also means that this generous plank of extra funding is not going to be much use to middle-income families. For some of these bursaries you don't have to be very rich not to qualify, as the income thresholds can be around £11,000 – which is for the combined income of both parents. So, to put it bluntly, some of these bursaries will not be much use if either of your parents has a full-time job.

Student responsibility

There is another subtle but important shift in the role of parents in student fee arrangements from 2006. Parents are often more worried than their student children about the financial burden. But the changes in the system of tuition fee repayment will shift more of the responsibility from the parents onto the shoulders of the students themselves. The fees might be higher, but they're going to be repaid out of the earnings of the student after they've left university or college, rather than borrowed from the Bank of Mum and Dad.

At present, under the current system which will end in 2005, tuition fees are means-tested, and about two-fifths of students do not get any subsidy – parents are expected to stump up the cash.

Under the new system, fees are rolled together with the student loan as something taken on by the student rather than their family. This is a trend that is likely to continue. Higher education is being presented as a sound financial investment, for the cost of which the student beneficiary is going to be expected to take responsibility, rather than being some kind of extended private education where the fees are paid by the parents.

Debt

What's also different about the system facing students arriving in 2006 will be the scale of the debt that will be built up. There has already been disquiet at how the current loan system leaves students with debts of around £12,000. But this is going to rise sharply again for the 2006 entry students, who will add the higher fees to their borrowing.

This gets back to the 'Is it worth it?' question. And it's a bit like asking someone if it's worth taking out a mortgage to buy a house. You might not want to commit yourself to such borrowing, but choosing not to get a mortgage and buy your own home also has its consequences. 'Is it worth it?' can soon translate into 'Do we really have any choice?'

Is a university or college education worth twice what it cost a few years ago? It's like asking whether a house is worth twice what it cost a few years ago. If you need a house, or if you want to go to university or college, it's almost irrelevant.

If the graduates of 2009 have run up debts of £20,000 to pay for their course at university or college, that's going to place a burden on their early years at work. But will repaying an interest-free loan, potentially over more than 20 years, keep them awake at night? In a culture that has grown increasingly comfortable with credit, the honest answer is probably not.

There has already been a cultural change towards debt, which allows us to borrow vast amounts of money to buy a house, way in excess of our savings – and student funding seems to be following behind. We borrow more and worry less.

A recurrent theme within students' own attitudes towards debt has been that, even though the amount they owe has continued to climb their own level of anxiety about it has lessened. And this is likely to reflect the fact that we're no longer shocked by the idea of students graduating with huge debts. It's become expected as part of the landscape.

A detailed survey of students in 2005 shows that in the past five years there has been an ongoing fall in the number of students who are 'seriously worried' about their level of debt. The figure currently stands at 10 per cent of students who agree strongly with the idea that they're worried about debts from university or college. This is much lower than might be expected and suggests that students won't be panicked by the forthcoming hike in fees.

Again, there are similarities with the US system, where students expect to pay large amounts of money for higher education and cover their costs with scholarships, loans and working their way through college. But in terms of costs, we're still on the nursery slopes, as there are universities in the United States where students are cheerfully paying $40,000 per year.

This has been described as a more 'transactional' system, where higher education is seen as a commodity to be bought, rather than an intellectual exercise which is valuable in its own right. If you're spending £9,000 on a degree course, will you have a different attitude to it than if you were spending £3,600?

When the first young people to experience this higher fee system start arriving in higher education institutions in 2006 they'll be watched carefully to see if consumer power has come to the campus.

4

Can parents afford it?

Parents often feel more worried about the financial aspect of university or college than their student offspring. They will have read about fees going up and students getting into debt and how much it costs to put a child through university or college. And they'll be thinking that when their children run out of cash it's going to be them, the parents, who provide the financial safety net.

It's a very confusing picture for many families. They want to support their children and help them into university or college, if that's what seems best for them. But the system of student finance is spectacularly opaque and it leaves parents worried about the scale of their financial commitment. Partly because it's means-tested, and partly because it's just a downright complicated system, it's hard for parents to get a clear view of how much they will have to contribute. It's like beginning the process of buying a house without ever being told the final asking price.

And what happens to students if their parents run out of money? Will they be able to finish? Is higher education going to leave a parent's fragile finances in complete ruins?

There's no doubt that many parents are going to have to part with cash when their children go to university or college. And if both parents are working in middle-income jobs, they're not going to get much financial assistance.

But the amounts that have to be paid are not going to mean taking out a second mortgage. At worst, it's going to be a few thousand a year, which is probably considerably cheaper than a new kitchen, arranging a wedding or buying a car. And it's not like paying mortgage repayments, where if you default there's a threatening letter in the post. Although many parents in practice pay more to their student children than they are required, if they didn't pay it would be a matter between the parent and child. There are no parental contribution police to come looking for unpaid money.

If the parents' combined income is below £22,010, they won't have to pay anything towards their children's higher education costs, and the full amount of student loan will be made available. But above that threshold parents will have to start contributing.

Your local education authority will be able to run the calculator over your exact payment requirement. It's a complicated formula that is based, broadly speaking, on parents having to contribute £1 for every £9.50 above the £22,010 threshold.

And if you are a parent wanting an immediate back of the envelope calculation about how much you'll have to pay, ignoring allowances and exceptions, work out how much you and your partner earn above £22,010. Then divide this figure by 9.5 and the result will be how much you have to pay.

For instance, if you earn £35,000, that works out at £1,367 per year.

But before getting too distracted by the maths, it's worth looking at the upper limit for payments. And for students in England starting in 2005, this is going to be the full tuition fee, £1,175, and 25 per cent of the maximum student loan, which in London is going to be £1,294. Put in simple terms, if parents have to pay the full amount it's going to cost £2,469. And below this figure will be a means-tested sliding scale of payments going down to zero.

If you do have to pay the maximum, it's a fair amount of extra money to find in a family budget, but it's not as cataclysmic as some parents seem to expect. However, parents will soon learn that you don't have to be that rich to have to pay this maximum amount. Two working parents with a combined income of about £42,720 would have to pay the full amount for a child at a university or college outside London.

The chapter on parental contributions has the details, but families' other financial obligations, such as other children at home, are also taken into account in the formula for how much parents have to contribute.

But the means-testing is still a fairly blunt instrument. It measures how much parents are earning but it's not going to take into account overall ability to pay. If your parents have moved house and taken on a big mortgage, you could be completely strapped for cash, while on paper having a decent income. And your financial support, or lack of it, will be determined by this income, even though in practice your parents might not be able to afford the required contributions.

The changes in the funding system for 2006 have been presented as relieving some of the financial burden from middle-income families, as parents will no longer have to pay towards tuition fees. Fees are becoming your responsibility, to be paid back, along with the student loans, when you leave higher education and begin work.

But the nagging fear will remain that if students are under-funded by the loan, parents will be expected to step in with the cash. This is certainly already happening to some extent. Surveys show that at least a quarter of students are receiving extra help from parents to pay for rent, food, books, clothes and to 'help out in a crisis'.

Of those who get help from parents, about a third get less than £500 per term, and about a fifth get between £500 and £1,000. At the top end of the handout spectrum, about a fifth get £1,500 or more from their parents each term. These are funds given by parents, rather than loans. And, interestingly, the habit of borrowing from parents seems to have reduced.

The average amount of money students have borrowed from parents is considerably lower now than in previous years. What could explain this is the corresponding increase in money owed on credit cards and hire purchase deals, which suggests that students are preferring to run up their own debts rather than turn to their parents.

This echoes research into how much parents contribute to student incomes, carried out by the Department for Education and Skills. This found that, between 1999 and 2003, the amount given by parents declined by 18 per cent, which again suggests that students are getting used to shouldering their own finances. The average student was receiving £1,300 from their family each year.

Nonetheless, there are examples of how far the protective instincts of parents can run, such as the survey a couple of years ago that found that mothers were using online supermarket services to send round fresh food to their student children.

And while parents worry about the actual money they have to hand over, they often overlook that their biggest contribution can be in the unseen subsidies, like food over the summer, or using a washing machine at the weekend. The family home is a kind of resource centre for students, saving them from buying all kinds of expensive equipment.

For parents earning a low income or no income, the picture of contributions is more straightforward. Bursaries, fees remission and full student loans are designed to provide the student with the extra financial support that might otherwise have come from parents. And for the student, this official funding, guaranteeing cash in hand, is probably preferable to having to inveigle money from a parent wrestling with their own financial problems.

Maybe in the longer term, if student finance remains in the same form for a number of years, parents will save up for sending their children to university or college or take out investments to stop students having to borrow so much.

But, at present, the funding system is in too much of a permanent revolution for anyone to have done that kind of financial planning. And parents will be left to worry about raising cash, when the evidence suggests that students are increasingly doing it for themselves.

5

How poor are students?

This might sound flippant, but it's a serious question. Because the decision about whether to go into higher education is often as much about perception as reality.

You hear young people saying that they don't want to go to university or college because they'll be so poor. And the image of the impoverished student is a long-standing stereotype, making people think about Young Ones-style students shivering in unheated houses, wearing second-hand clothes and living on a diet of own-brand baked beans and toast.

But is this really true any more? Students certainly owe a great deal of money, and that causes genuine hardship. They also don't have as much to spend as someone in full-time work. But is their lifestyle so awful? For many students, the evidence suggests that it isn't that bad at all.

And, even though it's not often said, a majority of today's students will be living much more comfortably than the Spartan living conditions of students in the 1970s or 1980s. Those students of yesteryear didn't have fees and big debts. But also they didn't have half the consumer expectations of today's students.

Almost a third of students have some access to a car during term-time. And about a fifth of students have their own car, usually bought for them by a parent.

This would have been unheard of 20 or 30 years ago. And students in those days would probably have had a meagre list of possessions in their rooms, with a radio cassette player passing for high technology.

> According to insurers and banks, today's students bring between £3,000 and £7,000 worth of possessions with them when they start university or college. A survey by the retailer, Marks and Spencer, put the average value of a student's possessions at £6,370.
>
> This includes laptops, widescreen televisions, DVD players, music systems, i-Pods, computer games, digital cameras and all the usual electronic gadgetry of a young person.

Clothes are also unlikely to be from straight off the rail at Oxfam. Students are sociable creatures, surrounded by other young people, and they are as likely to dress to impress as any other group of youngsters. So designer labels are far from unknown on campus.

You can get a glimpse of this lifestyle when you look at some of the rules about student residences, where there are stipulations about the size of fridge that students can bring with them. Because mini-fridges are where some students expect to keep their beer. And it suggests a picture of a student room where instead of a few old posters and a record player, there's enough stuff to fill the front window of an electrical shop.

Maybe this shouldn't surprise us. If you took any sample of predominantly middle-class teenagers, they would expect to have much of this accumulation of possessions. And students are no exception. It is very different from the picture of Pot Noodle-eating teenagers huddling over a bar heater for warmth that we associate with the idea of impoverished students.

Students themselves will say that such an average is distorted by the number of students who are able to rely on the lavish help of their parents. And they say that these affluent youngsters, whose new motors are clogging the campus car park, are unrepresentative of the majority who are struggling to survive on a threadbare loan.

There are social extremes in universities and colleges, as elsewhere. And the amount of support from parents, or the lack of it, can make a big difference to the comfort zones of student life. About a fifth of students get more than £1,500 per term in support from their parents.

But it's also the case that overall living standards and expectations have risen across the whole of society – and student life is no exception. Student accommodation isn't quite hotel standard, but compared to the frugality of old-style halls of residences, today's students are much better housed.

This also reflects institutions' need to attract students, their paying customers, and so decent halls of residence are part of the package. This includes rooms with en suite bathrooms, high-speed internet access, and halls with sports and fitness facilities. It probably wouldn't occur to students living in these halls that their predecessors a couple of decades before were sharing bathrooms and shower facilities.

So, how poor are students? They don't have much spending power, but all the surveys suggest that, pound for pound, they have more possessions than the average for their age group. Which is to say, they're not enduring terrible privations for their three years of studying.

This image of students laden with expensive gadgets might not seem to square with the stories of students struggling on a sub-subsistence income. But there could be some explanations for this, which also cast a wider light on student finance.

Many students work during term-time, and this hard-earned cash is going to be an important part of how they pay for a social life and consumer goods such as clothes and DVDs. Surveys of student incomes from the Department for Education and Skills show that students are now much more likely to be working and earning from part-time jobs. Income from students' jobs rose by 48 per cent between 1999 and 2003 – and the trends suggest that this will continue to be a significant part of students' financial support.

Also, many students have become accustomed to being deep in debt and, when you owe thousands, spending another couple of hundred might not seem that much extra, especially when the financial hangover won't kick in until after you've left university or college.

Old-style students didn't have many possessions in part because they didn't have any access to credit. Most bank managers in the 1970s and 1980s would have howled with laughter at the idea of lending thousands of pounds to a student. So, once the grant was gone, students did without. Now students live in a world of easy credit and they have the consumer goods and the credit card bills to prove it.

It's also worth remembering another practical detail. University and college terms are usually only 10 weeks and, since students are often working during the holidays, it's a fairly concentrated period of spending.

This view of relative affluence might not go down well with students currently at university or college, who probably don't feel for a moment that they're having it easy. But it's worth reassuring yourself if you are thinking about going into higher education that it won't be three years living on gruel and having less pocket money than a 12-year-old.

And without sounding like some kind of Victorian housekeeper, the cost of food is relatively inexpensive as a proportion of student expenditure. It's also worth noting that about a third of students receive support from parents to help with their food bills.

Even without parental hand-outs, living and eating healthily shouldn't be a problem. And, if students are living and eating unhealthily it's not a financial decision, as the evidence suggests that students on average are spending about the same each week on mobile phones as they are on food, and again a similar amount on clothes, which tells its own story about the student lifestyle.

But the trouble with asking how poor students are is that students can have very different experiences despite having similar incomes. If you're getting £5,000 or £6,000 per year from loans, part-time work and a little help from your family, you're not going to be well-off. But if you only need this cash for term-time and can rely on living cost-free with parents for the breaks, then it's going to be manageable, especially if the parental home is used as a base while earning more money over the summer.

But not all students have a parental support system to rely on, and surviving for three years on the loan and any other earnings is tough. And like anyone living on a low income, students are vulnerable to debt and a lack of cash for unexpected expenses, which can mean even more borrowing.

Even then, is temporary hardship the same thing as being poor? As George Orwell said, being poor isn't about not having anything today, it's about knowing you'll have nothing tomorrow. And for students, is that really the case?

6

Location, location, location: choosing a university or college

Variable fees

The idea behind introducing 'variable fees' (otherwise known as top-up or tuition fees) in 2006 was that they would be, er, variable. By this it was intended that, rather than a flat rate for tuition fees, there would be a whole range of charges, with different universities and colleges setting different fees in an attempt to attract students to their courses. And it was thought that there would be big discussions about whether students should pick a course that was cheaper, to save a few quid in the short term, or else opt for a more expensive course which might prove a cannier long-term investment.

But this was a dog that didn't bark. Almost all courses at all universities and colleges are going to have the same £3,000 price tag. So, whether you're taking a vocational-style degree in tourism studies at a new university or studying classics at a venerable Oxbridge college, there is every chance that the fee will be the same.

This neatly kicks one set of arguments about price and quality into touch. And, to be honest, picking a course on price would never have been a particularly smart move. If you want to study a subject because you're good at it and you like it, it would be a fairly dim move to opt for another course you didn't like and weren't very good at because the fees were a few quid cheaper.

Even though fees have grabbed all the headlines, they're only a minority part of the cost of going into higher education and in future won't be paid up front, so they really should never have been a serious factor in choosing a course. But, at least in the immediate future, such questions have been rendered irrelevant by almost everyone charging the same fee.

Bursaries

The same uniformity does not apply to bursaries, which are the grants to be paid out directly by universities and colleges from 2006. These look set to range from £1,000 to £5,000 and so could become a reason for a student to choose one university or college over another.

It might not be enough to entirely shape a decision about what to study, but if two institutions were offering similar courses, and held equal attractions, then it's quite possible that students would be drawn by the prospect of the cash.

Salary potential

Another hardy perennial is the idea that some courses are going to lead to more lucrative careers than others. This might be the case. For instance, this year's graduates are expected to find a strong demand for accountants, whose starting salaries will be driven up accordingly.

But anyone applying for accountancy will need to want to study it and have an aptitude for the subject. It's not the sharpest move to pursue a course you don't like because of a brief mark-up on starting salaries. And in three years time there might be a glut of accountants and the demand might be for IT graduates.

There are courses that will plainly lead to better-paid jobs. If you go into a specific professional training, such as dentistry or medicine, you might eventually expect a comfortable living after you've qualified.

But many big employers will say that they want talented people with good degrees, almost regardless of the subject. And laying precise career plans at the ages of 17 and 18, when school pupils are applying for university or college, can be jumping the gun.

Employment league tables

There are elaborate league tables showing which universities and colleges have produced the graduates who are most quickly employed, and which imply that this is a league table of universities from which you're most likely to get a job. But these can be very misleading. At the top of these tables there is usually a far from prestigious institution, while long-established colleges are languishing far below.

But what this really means is that students from the more eminent universities and colleges haven't rushed into jobs, might have travelled or taken time off, and are planning their next move. And cynics might say that the wealthier social intake might mean that more of these students can afford not to go straight into work.

Universities and colleges that do extremely well in these employability tables might often have a higher proportion of less well-off students taking vocational courses, who might be expected to get a job as soon as possible after graduation. So be cautious about the idea that there is some kind of equation for finding the course and institution which will deliver the biggest bucks after graduation.

Local costs

But in terms of minimizing the cost, the geographical location of a university or college is going to have an influence. Different cities have different prices for accommodation, going out in the evening and everyday stuff like food, clothes and taxis home. And over the course of three years this is going to add up to a considerable difference in spending.

There will be some obvious examples. If you want to live in an up-market part of London it's going to be pricier than a bargain-basement area of a northern city. But if you're less certain about the likely cost, then check out some estate agent websites in the areas in which you're considering. The biggest cost is going to be rent and you'll soon get a feel for the price ranges.

Don't necessarily assume that a big city like London will always work out to be more expensive, because as well as the cost of living there's also the question of earning a living. Most students are going to have part-time jobs during term time to supplement their loans and to reduce borrowing. And the greater availability of temporary work in a big city is likely to offset at least some of the higher costs. Students in London can also claim a larger loan than elsewhere, up to £5,175 compared to £4,195.

If you're really getting into researching a university or college in terms of the location, rather than the course, it's also worth looking at the practicalities such as local transport and where you could get your shopping. If you have to travel everywhere by taxi and the only shop is a gourmet delicatessen, it's going to be an expensive three years.

It should be the course and the institution that you're choosing, rather than the postcode. But it's certainly the case that the threat of higher costs and debts are influencing where people are going to university or college. The most conspicuous example of this is the increasing number of students who remain at home while they are at university or college.

Living at home

The loans available to students who are living at home with their parents are smaller than those away from home. But nonetheless living at home is going to mean a substantial financial saving. Rent is the biggest cost and so staying in that old bedroom is going to cut this major expense out of the budget. There are also all kinds of subsidies due to being at home, such as access to electricity, telephone and the contents of the fridge.

There is anecdotal evidence to suggest that staying at home while at university or college is becoming particularly common among students at some of the inner-city universities and colleges with a less well off student population. These students, who might be the first in their family to have gone into higher education, do not assume that going to university or college means three years of campus capers in a location as far away as possible.

For students from low-income families, staying at home could almost mean leaving university or college with little or no debt. If they qualify for grants and bursaries they can cover the cost of fees – and if they're working part time they can cover the costs of the course and a social life.

The student loan, which represents most of student debt, is mostly going to cover rent, bills and food. And if a student can cut down on these expenses by staying at home, then it's going to be a very affordable route to getting a degree. The downside of this is that the choice of universities and colleges and courses is narrowed because, even if you live in a major city, there are still not going to be a vast number of universities or colleges within commutable distance.

Parents' investment property

At the other end of the income scale, another approach to cutting the cost of going into higher education has been for parents to buy a flat in the location where their offspring is studying. For wealthier families who are not going to get much financial assistance, and who are going to have to pay their son or daughter's accommodation costs, it has often been as cheap to buy a flat and pay the mortgage, rather than rent.

This became quite a common practice when house prices were soaring and buy-to-let investors were at their most bullish. It enabled a parent to turn the cost of a child at university or college into an investment, with a profit to be made on the property by selling at the end of the three years. The problem is that such schemes only really work when the property market is buoyant, and when prices are stagnating it's a much less attractive prospect. For a parent to buy a flat that depreciates in value for three years would only compound the expense of sending their child to university or college.

With all these considerations it's important to remember what it is you want to get out of university or college. And even though it's sensible to avoid unnecessary debt and expense, that can't be the most important factor in where you choose to go to study.

Like buying a house, it's not just a case of getting the very cheapest place available, it's about finding somewhere in which you'll feel comfortable and which fits in with your ambitions. The cost is important, but the location has to be somewhere with enough room for a view of the future.

7

Winners and losers

Let's be honest. When people are worrying about student finance, what they fear is that they'll have got themselves into ruinous debt without gaining a qualification that's worth the stress and expense. The confusion over higher charges has prompted fears that people will lose out, in the same way that they might be afraid of a dubious type of mortgage or insurance.

Who are the real winners and losers going to be in the higher education stakes?

Middle-income families with two working parents might have a justifiable grouse that they'll end up feeling more of the financial pain. You don't have to be very rich to be considered too rich to get any support. Under the current system, parents with a combined income above £45,000 are going to get no help with fees and will have to pay the maximum parental contribution. This puts a couple of primary school teachers into the same payment bracket as Paul McCartney.

While genuinely rich parents are rich enough not to worry about a little extra expense, and poor parents are going to get assistance, it'll be the middle-income families who will get squeezed. In terms of value for money, both the rich and poor families can approach the arrangements with some optimism.

Wealthy families

Under the 2006 arrangements, students from wealthy families are still only paying the same fees as everyone else. And, since they are all subsidized, the rich student is still getting a higher education at below the actual cost. If you are a parent who has been sending a child to private school, then the shift to university or college will mean saving money because the fees for most private schools are well in excess of university or college tuition fees.

Regardless of income, three-quarters of the student loan is available to everyone, which means that well-off families can still benefit from an interest-free advance. And don't forget that, in some of the most competitive universities and colleges, almost half the undergraduates come from private schools – so for all these families the university and college funding arrangements are going to seem like a bargain.

Poorer families

At the lower end of the income scale, there are also reasons for confidence. Working-class students have been woefully under-represented in universities and colleges, and much of the new-look funding system is shaped around encouraging more students from poorer backgrounds to apply. The incentives in terms of grants and bursaries are targeted at low-income families, who are being offered the chance to send their children to university or college at virtually no expense. While middle-class students will be piling up the debt, poorer students will have grants and bursaries to avoid much of this borrowing.

Whether this financial tactic works, or whether resistance to higher education proves a more complex cultural attitude, will not be known for years. But for any students from low-income families who take the plunge, there is plenty of evidence to suggest that the student support system is stacked up in their favour.

And, in many ways, students from low-income backgrounds stand to win the most from the chance to have a heavily subsidized three years in higher education, rather than the quick buck of going into work.

Student confidence

Students themselves seem to think that they are going to win from their investment. According to the Unite/Mori poll of student attitudes, 89 per cent of students currently in higher education agree or strongly agree that the money spent is a good investment. That's a fairly resounding vote of confidence and is supported by 81 per cent of students saying that university or college will have set them in 'good stead' for their working lives. And most of these angst-free youngsters do not feel under pressure to 'succeed and make money'.

This is one of the more detailed annual surveys of student life and it does project a picture of students who are satisfied with their decision to go to university or college – with 83 per cent optimistic about their employment prospects when they graduate. The survey also records the less easy to specify skills that students believe they will have gained from going to university or college.

The largest number of students point to 'self-confidence' as being a key benefit from university or college, along with the ability to work under pressure, and organizational skills. These can be hard to quantify on a balance sheet of profit and loss, but for these young people these particular qualities are extremely important. And when thinking about what's won and lost in the decision to go into higher education, such life skills should not be overlooked.

Also, if you're looking for candidates for the winners' and losers' enclosures, you have to consider the price of not going to university or college. Despite the increased cost and despite their complaints, middle-income families from middle England will continue to encourage their children to go into higher education. You don't need to have a crystal ball to know that or to see why.

By going to university or college you know that you will be in a stronger position to pursue your chosen career than if you leave education at 16 or 18. In the jobs market, the degree remains the key to higher status and higher-income jobs. It might not be fair, and there might be exceptions, but graduates have so far shown no sign of relinquishing their grip on the sought-after jobs.

The approaching increase in fees might seem radical and might give your parents some sleepless nights. But if you take a wider international perspective, you can see how far the middle classes will go to get their children into those graduation photos.

In the United States, despite eye-wateringly high costs there's more competition than ever for university and college places. With the decline of skilled blue-collar jobs in manufacturing in the US it's become even more important for youngsters to qualify for professional and hi-tech graduate jobs. There are forecasts of a more polarized workforce in the US, with graduates filling the high-quality, well-paid jobs, while non-graduates are increasingly stuck with insecure, badly-paid service sector jobs.

There are already countries in Europe where considerably more than a majority of young people, particularly women, go to university or college. In Iceland 80 per cent of female school-leavers now go into higher education. And this raises questions about the job prospects of the minority who don't go.

It's not meant to be a sales pitch for going into higher education, but the old argument that getting a few years' work experience is as good as getting a degree increasingly sounds like more of a risky gamble.

You can leave school at 16 and have 'won' an advantage by earning money at the first opportunity and avoiding debt. But five years later, when students of the same age as you are leaving university and college, the rates of pay are going to swing heavily in favour of the graduate. If you can cope with the short-term hardship and borrowing, then it has to be asked 'What's to be lost by going to university or college?'

8

What does that mean?

Access to Learning Fund

This is a safety net for students facing some kind of financial emergency. It's administered through the higher education institution rather than the local authority and is intended to plug any gap left by other grants.

Bursaries

These are grants given by individual universities and colleges to students. From 2006, bursaries are going to be much more widespread, as institutions are obliged to show that they are making efforts to recruit more widely and to support students from less well-off communities. There is no fixed figure, but it's likely to be somewhere between £300 and £5,000 per year. And, best of all, these do not have to be paid back.

These bursaries are going to be targeted at specific groups, such as students from low-income families, local students or those with high grades. Every university and college will have its own priority.

Gap year

This applies to students who take a year out after leaving school and so do not start university or college in the autumn after their A level exams. These students, who have places offered for university or college in 2005 but who will not start until 2006, are going to be allowed to go through under the old fees system rather than be charged the incoming higher rate.

Even though they are starting in 2006, and other students will be paying the higher tuition fees, the gap year cohort will have their three years under the old system. This means that the last of the 'up-front' fees students will have passed through the system in 2009–10.

Graduate endowment

This is the system in Scotland in which former students pay back something towards the cost of their higher education, with payments made when students have graduated and are working. The idea is that it provides an endowment for future students.

Grants

Making a comeback, but not in the form that parents might remember. These grants are part of the 2006 overhaul of student finance and are intended to counterbalance the higher tuition fees. They'll be worth up to £2,700, won't have to be repaid, and will be awarded depending on a means test of parents' income. Not to be confused with student loans, which replaced old-style grants as support for covering living costs.

Income contingent

Another way of saying that financial assistance is a means-tested calculation dependent on how much money is earned in a house-hold. For student support, it's usually based on the combined income of both parents.

Independent student

This isn't a state of mind, but a label to describe students who are no longer the financial responsibility of their parents. This could be because they are mature students, they've supported themselves for several years, their parents are no longer alive, or there has been a permanent loss of contact with parents.

'New' university

This usually describes a university that was once a polytechnic. The conversion of polytechnics into universities took place in 1992, so 'new' is an increasingly out-of-date label. Slightly older universities, also founded in the 20th century, are often labelled 'redbrick'. And the most prestigious universities are known as Russell Group universities.

Overseas students

Also known as international students, these are students who come to study in the United Kingdom from other countries. These students pay higher fees than UK students – and the maximum upper limit for fees does not apply for them. However, students from other European Union countries do not count as overseas students – these students pay the same tuition fees as UK students.

Part-time students

This can be any type of student who is not studying full time on a course. They can be studying for the same degree as full-time students, but are spreading the course over a longer stretch of time. Many part-time students have full-time jobs, by contrast with full-time students who often have part-time jobs. Part-time students can claim support and will have to pay fees, but both are at separate rates from full-time students.

Scholarship

This is another way of describing a grant given to a student, either by the university or by another sponsoring body. The often-blurred distinction between a bursary and a scholarship is that a bursary is usually dependent on income while a scholarship is usually dependent on academic achievement.

Student loan

This term usually refers to the loan provided for students by the official lending organization, the Student Loans Company. This loan is meant to cover living costs such as rent, food and bills. It's paid at the beginning of term and the amount that you receive depends on your income or your parents' incomes.

This student loan is interest free and is repaid in monthly instalments once you have finished university or college and are earning the equivalent of £15,000 per year. This loan, from the Student Loans Company, should not be confused with loans made to students by banks and other commercial lenders. These will charge interest, and repayments will be fixed regardless of earnings.

Tuition fees

These are fees paid by a student as a contribution towards the cost of higher education. When they were introduced in 1998 they sparked protests from students and controversy has continued to surround them. From 2006 the fees will increase sharply to an upper limit of £3,000 per year.

They are also known as variable fees and top-up fees. As 'variable' implies, these fees are not fixed but can be set by universities and colleges at any rate between zero and £3,000. Unfortunately for students, almost all courses seem set to be priced at £3,000.

Students starting in autumn 2005 will have to pay the annual tuition fee of £1,175 at the beginning of the year. From autumn 2006, they will have to pay back the annual fee of up to £3,000 after they have graduated and are working.

Up-front fees

This piece of jargon describes the requirement to pay the tuition fee before starting a course. You might see information saying that 'up-front fees are being abolished'. This is about the change in repayments for tuition fees in 2006, when up-front fees are replaced by a system in which repayments are made after graduation.

Welsh Assembly Learning Grant

Funding for Welsh students from less well-off families. It's not a loan and doesn't need to be paid back.

Young Students' Bursary

A means-tested, non-repayable grant available for Scottish students. It's aimed at supporting young people from lower-income families, with 'young' defined as 25 or under.

Part Two

Financial support for students

Finance for vocational courses

Over the last 17 years, Career Development Loan have helped tens of thousands of people to give their careers a lift. Whilst you can't use a Career Development Loan to pay for a three or four year university undergraduate course, it could help you to cover the cost of a vocational course of up to two years. You can also include a further year's practical experience if it is part of the course.

So how do they work? Well it's simple really. You borrow between £300 and £8,000 to help pay for your training from a Career Development Loan provider such as The Co-operative Bank. You don't need to be a customer already to apply.

The Department for Education and Skills then pays the interest on your Career Development Loan while you are learning and for up to one month afterwards. After that, you repay the loan over an agreed period of up to five years, at a rate of interest that was fixed before you started the course.

For example, say you are applying for a 12 month course which starts on 1 October 2005. You don't pay anything until 1 December 2006 as the government pays the interest for you. After that, you pay off your loan over the agreed period of 1 to 5 years.

To find out more about a Career Development Loan from The Co-operative Bank, simply phone **08457 212 212**, call into your local branch or visit our website on **www.co-operativebank.co.uk**

Your payments remain fixed when the loan is agreed. Interest-free for up to one month after the end of the course. You pay back nothing until two months after the course is complete. You can repay the loan over a period of 12 to 60 months.

Applicants must be UK resident and aged between 18 and 69 years of age.

Credit facilities are provided by The Co-operative Bank p.l.c. (Registered No. 990937), Head Office, P.O. Box 101, 1 Balloon Street, Manchester M60 4EP and are subject to status. The Bank reserves the right to decline any application or offer a loan at a rate that differs from any advertised. Calls may be monitored and/or recorded for security and/or training purposes.

The Co-operative Bank is authorised and regulated by the Financial Services Authority (No. 121885), subscribes to the Banking Code, is a member of the Financial Ombudsman Service and is licensed by the Office of Fair Trading (No. 006110).

9

Financial support for students

How much?

If you're trying to work out how much it's going to cost to go to university or college, then there are two questions to consider. First, how much will you have to pay out? And, second, how much financial support will you be given?

Whether you're an optimist who wants to look first at the size of grant you might receive, or a pessimist who wants to look at how much you'll pay in fees, you'll still need to look at both sides of the equation. It's a system of checks and balances, with expenses and subsidies offsetting one another depending on your family circumstances.

Funding changes

The student funding system is in the process of major changes, with new support and higher fees being introduced in 2005 and 2006. And, more than ever, anyone trying to fathom the complexities of student finance will need to look at what is being offered in support and what is being charged.

While there have been loud arguments about the forthcoming hike in tuition fees to £3,000 per year, to make sense of this figure you have to ask what's being made available to cover this increased cost. The answer, rather infuriatingly, is 'that depends', because the system of student support is means-tested. The amount available will be determined by the income of your family. Another unknown element to introduce is the amount that students might be offered by individual universities or colleges, as many are in the process of developing bursary schemes.

We're following the path of the optimists, by looking first at what support is available to students. This might overlap in places with chapters on what university or college is going to cost, because the subject areas are interwoven. But, taken together, they should provide a picture of the size of the cheque you'll be writing out to pay for higher education.

Where to apply for financial support

With so many types of support, the question of where to apply can also seem confusing. And there is no real one-stop shop for support.

But there are a number of key contacts who will be responsible for most of the support available. The local education authority (which is the education department of the local council) will have information and forms and will be the channel for applications such as the means-tested loans.

The payment and repayment of these loans is administered by the Student Loans Company, which will send support such as grants or fee payments direct to the student's bank account or to the institution. Forms can also be downloaded directly from a useful website, Student Finance Direct (www.studentsupportdirect.co.uk), which also has information and advice for further contacts. This includes detailed guides to specific types of support, such as for students with children or with disabilities.

Bursaries and other emergency hardship grants are arranged through the individual universities and colleges.

When to apply

With respect to when to apply for support the general rule is: the sooner the better. You don't need to wait to get a confirmed place on a course before applying (because that mightn't happen until after the A level results, when there's only a brief breathing space before the start of the academic year).

You can return the form to the local education authority as soon as you have a clear idea about where you're likely to be going – and if that changes, you can supply the new details later. But at least you'll have got the ball rolling and they will have details about you, the student, and your family's income.

It's also useful to open a bank account in advance so that there is somewhere into which the cheque can be paid at the start of term.

The deadline for applications for financial support for new students is July 1st. But if you miss this you can still qualify for support – there's just no guarantee it will be available at the very beginning of term. The final cut-off for applying is nine months after the beginning of the course.

Once you have sent back the application form, with all the supporting evidence required, it is expected to take six to eight weeks to be processed, after which you will be told how much support you can receive.

10

Student loans

Living expenses

Despite all the sound and fury about tuition fees, the biggest cost facing students is in keeping themselves housed, fed and clothed during their years at university or college. Basic living costs are going to be much more expensive than tuition fees – and when students graduate with mountainous debts, the largest part of these will have been from mundane expenditure on rent and bills.

Interest-free loans

To cover these costs, you can take out loans that are, effectively, interest free. The repayment takes into account inflation, so the money paid back will be slightly higher than the amount borrowed, but there is no charge for interest added. These student loans, or student maintenance loans as they are sometimes called, are administered by the Student Loans Company – and are not to be confused with commercial loans from banks or other lenders.

And whenever you read about 'student loans' it will usually mean these official, subsidized loans – paid out to students in termly instalments when they're studying, and then repaid by students when they've graduated.

But how large a student loan can you borrow?

The maximum amounts available, depending on parental income, are:

- students living away from home at a London university or college: £5,175;
- students living away from home at a university or college outside London: £4,195;
- students living at home: £3,320.

The final academic year is counted as having fewer weeks than the first and second years, and the final year loans are lower:

- students living away from home at a London university or college: £4,490;
- students living away from home at a university or college outside London: £3,645;
- students living at home: £2,900.

The minimum amounts available, regardless of parental income, are:

- students living away from home at a London university or college: £3,370;
- students living away from home at a university or college outside London: £3,145;
- students living at home: £2,490.

The final academic year is counted as having fewer weeks than the first and second years, and the final year loans are lower:

- students living away from home at a London university or college: £3,370;
- students living away from home at a university or college outside London: £2,735;
- students living at home: £2,175.

This probably looks like too many numbers at once. But the most commonly quoted amount will be £4,195 per year, which is the maximum amount of loan available for a student living away from home at a university or college outside London. It's the kind of loan that will be given to a student whose parents are not earning more than £32,745 per year.

So, before disappearing into a blizzard of numbers, it's worth stepping back and recognizing that all the loan amounts for students will be somewhere on a sliding scale between these two amounts, £5,175 and £2,490.

Maximum and minimum loans

At the highest level, for students living away from home at a London university or college, from a low-income background, the maximum loan is £5,175. At the very lowest level, for students who live at home with their well off parents and go to a university or college outside London, the figure would be £2,490.

And the factors that will influence the amount are: more for living away from home, more for studying in London and more for coming from a low-income family. If you can get three out of three, you'll qualify for the full loan.

But just to add another complication, the whole loan isn't means-tested. The first 75 per cent is available to students regardless of how rich or poor their parents might be. So everyone can borrow this amount.

But there is an additional 25 per cent of the loan that is means tested. The less money a student's family earns, the more of this 25 per cent they will be able to claim as a loan. For students at a non-London university or college whose parents earn up to £42,720, there will be some part of this 25 per cent of loan available.

As an example, if a student leaves home to go to a higher education institution, and it's outside London, the loan available to all students will be £3,145. For students from lower-income families, there will be another 25 per cent, which brings it up to the £4,195. This means that, between students at this out-of-London university or college, there's a possible difference of about £35 per week between the maximum loan and the minimum.

If a student is living away from home and studying at a London university or college, then the minimum amount per year available is £3,880. With the additional 25 per cent means-tested loan, this can be brought up to £5,175. For these loan figures, 'London' means any of the University of London colleges and any other higher education institution within the Metropolitan police area. There's no extra benefit for students who live at home with their parents when that home is in London. Wherever the location, the maximum loan for students living at home is £3,320.

Loans for non-standard length courses

There are variations in the loans available where courses are of non-standard lengths. For instance, if courses stretch beyond 30 weeks per year, there is an additional weekly loan available, up to £75 per week for students outside London and £96 per week in London. And all the amounts for annual loans are reduced for a student's final year. For example, outside London, the maximum loan for a final year student is £3,645 rather than £4,195 for a first year.

Paying back the loan

It's worth emphasizing that all these amounts of money are not grants being handed out but are loans which are being made available, interest-free. They will have to be paid back when you have graduated and are working.

This does not mean that it's obligatory to take out a loan. If you're fortunate enough not to need this financial support, then there is no requirement to apply.

There are, inevitably, some financial wise guys who say that if you're rich enough not to need the student loan while at university or college, it's still effectively an interest-free advance for three years. And if you were going to do something like buy a car, the student loan becomes a very efficient form of finance. But, in practice, student loans are going to be necessary for most students. And the loan will be the basic building block of paying your way through university or college.

Parental contributions

Built into the loan calculation is the assumption that most working parents will also be putting their hands into their pockets to support their children at university or college. The means-tested element of the loan – representing 25 per cent of the maximum amount – is where the parents are meant to work out their expected contribution.

Parents at the lower end of the income scale, earning a combined income of below £22,010, will not be expected to contribute anything to the upkeep of their student children. But, above that amount, parents will be expected to contribute on a sliding scale depending on their income.

For a student outside London living away from home, parents will be expected to contribute towards living costs on a sliding scale anywhere between zero and the maximum £1,050. To be at the top end, families have to earn £42,720.

The way this is worked out is that the first amount of parental contribution covers the tuition fee – up to the full £1,175. This maximum fee liability equates to an income of £32,745. If there is more parental contribution liable to be paid above this, this is then deducted from the student loan available.

For London students, the top of the parental income threshold is higher, at £45,048. This means that students with parents with a combined income below this figure will get some extra loan.

Using the student funding see-saw system, as the amount of means-tested parental contribution goes down, so the student loan available goes up. The theory is that all students end up with similar amounts of financial support. Poorer students have access to higher levels of student loans; richer students have higher levels of parental contributions.

Reality check

But let's put away the ready reckoner for a second and allow in a little chilly reality. When we're talking about financial support available to students from their parents, the official version can be a long way from what really happens. First, the level of financial support available to students takes into account parental income. But it doesn't take into account lousy parents who won't cough up.

There isn't a student loans police force that can make parents pay their means-tested required contribution. And if they don't pay their fair share, then the student's income goes down and the Student Loans Company won't make up the difference.

On the other side of the coin, you'll hear parents complaining that the official levels of parental contribution are just a starting point and that they really pay a much higher amount. Even if they don't hand over more cash each term, parents provide a major source of subsidy for students. Driving a student to and from university or college might save a big train fare, lending them a portable television will save a few quid, and putting them on the family insurance might reduce a student's running costs.

Parents might also put up the cash for a returnable deposit on rented accommodation, or help students with money before they even go to university or college, such as getting books or a computer. For many students this back-up is going to be an important financial safety net. It won't appear in any balance sheet, but it shouldn't be overlooked, because it's quite likely to exceed the formal amount of parental contribution.

What does a student loan cover?

The student loan and the means-tested parental contribution, worth up to £5,175 per year in London, are meant to pay everyday living expenses. The biggest single cost is likely to be rent, plus the whole range of expenses facing anyone living independently, such as food, phone bills, gas, electricity and clothes.

This loan is also meant to cover entertainment, leisure and going out. Which is likely to mean, going out cheaply. It is also going to fund your course-related expenses, such as text books, equipment and the usual stationery cupboard stuff.

But there is no one checking up on how you spend this money. It's usually paid in three instalments, at the beginning of each term, and how you use the cash is your own responsibility. After all, this is a loan, not a gift, and you're going to be paying it back for many years after you've graduated. If you blow it all on a dubious suit in the first week, no one is going to come round and ask for the money back. But, also, no one is going to offer any more.

How do you get a student loan?

Student loans, usually paid directly into a bank account, are provided by the Student Loans Company. But the application process, for students in England, is most likely to begin with the local education authority (often abbreviated to LEA). This is part of your local council and they have the application forms that will trigger the loans and the means-testing process.

Once you've returned the application form, you will be told the size of the student loan you will be able to borrow and how much your parents will have to pay. You can also use a website for this application process: www.studentfinancedirect.co.uk.

Whether you apply through the local authority or the website, there are calls for students not to leave these applications too late, or else they risk not having their loan cheques ready at the start of term.

The current timetable allows students to put in their application forms from March, with the closing deadline being the beginning of July. Applications after this will be processed, but might not be ready for when courses begin in the autumn.

Tuition fee support

The spectre of higher tuition fees has become one of the most contro-versial areas of student finance. But let's try to get a clearer picture of what it will really mean if you are planning to go to university or college – and of the support put in place to balance the cost.

Students starting in 2005

Although there is a fixed tuition fee of £1,175 for all full-time courses, not everyone will actually pay this amount. In fact, only about two in five students will pay the full amount. This is because the fee is assessed alongside the income of the student and the student's parents – and students from less well-off families will have their fees paid for them. About two in five students won't pay anything at all – and the remainder will pay a reduced fee.

For 2005, if the combined income of your parents is less than £22,010, you will not have to pay any tuition fee. If your parents earn anything between £22,010 and £32,744, then you will have to pay a proportion of the tuition fee. And if your parents' income is above £32,744, then you are liable for the full fee.

For those students who are assessed as being eligible for support for their fees, the money is paid directly to the university or college.

To get this financial support, don't wait until your exam results in the summer – apply as soon as you have a good idea of where you will be studying. If this changes later, you can inform the local education authority. The opening time for applications for financial support is usually March.

Application forms are available from your local education authority, usually through the student awards officer. Or you can get advice from a national helpline: 0800 731 9133. Information and application forms are also available through the website: www.studentfinancedirect.co.uk.

You will need your National Insurance number for the application. If you've lost it and need a replacement, contact the Inland Revenue on 0845 915 7006.

Students starting in autumn 2006

Tuition fees – and the support to help pay for them – are going to increase for students beginning courses in autumn 2006. This is going to be a substantial increase in cost – up to £3,000 per year – which means £9,000 for a three-year degree course.

But the first point to make, and it's worth repeating, is that the new system will also change how repayments are made. Instead of paying up-front at the beginning of the year, repayments of tuition fees are going to be deferred until after students have graduated. It's not exactly extra funding, because you're still paying back more money, but it means there won't be the same financial pinch-point at the entry point to higher education. And it does represent a three-year interest-free advance of the money to cover the fees.

The fees, up to the full £9,000 for three years, will be deducted from a graduate's salary each month, until it's paid off. And if after 25 years the debt still hasn't been cleared, it's written off. So, maybe in a few decades from now, some ne'er do well fortysomethings will be celebrating.

Repayments

Fee repayments are going to be rolled into the repayments for student loans – and, in effect, it's going to be a bigger student loan, except technically speaking – part is going to be for tuition fees and the rest for the student loan. But in practical terms the two repayments – for tuition fees and loans – will be merged. There will be a single payment each month for both fees and loans.

This might sound like it's getting more complicated than the degree course you'll be studying but, in practice, it means you can stop worrying about paying tuition fees until you've graduated and are working. There is a fee, it exists, it's up to £3,000, but for you, the student, there won't be any cheque to hand over.

For the purposes of explaining the support available, the figure that's quoted for the new fees system is £3,000 per year. This is a maximum figure, rather than a fixed amount, and in theory universities and colleges could charge less for all or some of their courses. But at the time of writing, the indications are that most universities and colleges will charge the maximum £3,000 for all courses, with few exceptions likely to emerge. And while the government says there will be no increase from £3,000 for several years, the institutions themselves are already warning that this maximum is set too low and that there needs to be flexibility for a higher fee.

Nonetheless, for the individual student, the aim will be to pay as little as possible and to get as much financial support as possible.

And to balance the £3,000 in fees, the government is introducing a means-tested, non-repayable grant worth up to £2,700. There are so far no exact figures for income levels needed to get the full amount, but the government says that about half of students will qualify for some of this grant. This grant will mean that the extra cost of the £3,000 fee will be offset, for those who qualify, by a slightly smaller grant.

There's an element of smoke and mirrors about this, because at the moment students from lower-income families simply have the tuition fee paid for them, with the subsidy moving invisibly from the government to the higher education institution. Under the new regulations, there isn't a subsidy as such, but there is to be a grant for a similar amount to the fees, which allows the generosity of the government to become a more visible affair.

And the shortfall of £300 is tidied up by the expectation that universities and colleges themselves will operate bursary schemes, offering extra support to students from low-income families.

For the individual student, the final balance sheet on tuition fees will depend on this means-tested grant. If they get some or all of the £2,700, then the impact of the increase in fees will be greatly softened.

But if you have to pay the full amount, then it might be a more muted benefit that the fees won't have to be paid back until after university or college.

12

Bursaries

Even though they haven't had the same kind of coverage as tuition fees, bursaries are becoming a significant part of the changing landscape of higher education. This development is likely to mean that some students will be getting twice as much financial support from the university or college than from the official grant – and, as the two will be added together, it could mean students from poorer backgrounds collecting £5,000 to £7,000 per year in non-repayable funding.

Without much attention being paid, universities and colleges across the country are beginning to announce plans for supporting students with particular financial needs. There have always been bursaries, with donations left by various worthies to help a small number of deserving cases. But the new wave of bursaries will be on a much bigger scale and will be more like those in the United States, where high levels of fees are offset with scholarships.

This isn't government money like the higher education grant, this is the university's or college's money, recycled from tuition fees and offered directly to students. At the most basic level, the bursaries will bridge the £300 gap between the upper level of the higher education grant, £2,700, and the maximum tuition fee, £3,000.

But there are signs that universities and colleges are being much more ambitious about the amounts they want to make available. This isn't just generosity from the institutions – the offer of a large bursary is becoming a recruitment tool to help them draw the most talented students.

There are already universities and colleges that are planning to offer extra cash for students with all A grades in their A levels, using the bursary as a straightforward cash offer to attract high-flyers. It's also not widely recognized that bursaries are going to be much more than a minor addition to government funding – with bursaries announced that are much larger than the maximum level of the government grant.

It's difficult to generalize about how much the average bursary is going to be worth, because every university and college will have its own arrangements. But there have already been announcements of bursaries worth between £3,000 and £5,000 per year. In most cases the bursaries will be used to encourage students who otherwise might not have entered higher education, particularly those from poorer backgrounds who have traditionally been under-represented.

There isn't any national plan for such bursaries, other than that some of the fee income should be put back into this kind of support. But it's worth researching what's on offer, because universities and colleges are pumping millions of pounds into them. And look beyond the headline figure, because the bursaries can be multi-layered.

There might be a fixed allowance for all students from families below a certain income threshold – and then a separate allowance might be available for such students who are from the local area or who reach a certain academic level. These might be able to be added together – and they won't count against any other student loans or grants. And, while the government wanted a market to emerge in the level of fees, in practice the emerging market is in bursaries, with considerable slices of money available to students.

So far it has tended to be the more prestigious universities and colleges that have announced their plans, with something of a bidding war to get the biggest headline figure. There is even an annual bursary of £10,000 at one institution for a small number of outstanding applicants.

The reason it has been the more established universities and colleges that have made the first moves on bursaries could reflect a couple of political realities. These institutions want to show that they're not socially exclusive – and these large bursaries are a public display of their readiness to support talented students from poorer backgrounds. It's also the case that these prestigious universities and colleges are often wealthier and have access to rich donors – and they have the capacity to put more cash into bursaries. What remains to be seen is how bursary offers will differ for the less famous universities and colleges and whether they will be able to afford to be as generous.

And this will undoubtedly play a part in where students apply to university or college. Getting an extra £10,000 for a three-year course is going to have a big impact in reducing loans and preventing the credit cards turning into a disaster zone.

How will such attractions compare with a different strategy, such as lowering tuition fees by £1,000 for all courses as one university is proposing? Will such a discount be less attractive than the offer of £1,000 in the hand as a bursary? It's the same amount of money, but packaged differently.

These are uncertain waters for higher education institutions, with students in the next few years being the first guinea pigs. And, if bursaries are a big crowd-puller, then they will have an impact on how universities and colleges sell themselves to students. Certainly, a no-strings-attached bursary has attractions for students. Bursaries do not have to be paid back and there is unlikely to be any scrutiny over how they are spent, so, for students who receive them, bursaries could feel like the rich relative they never had.

But rather like the distribution of rich relatives, there could be complaints that, if bursaries become a significant part of the student support structure, it could become a bit of a lottery as to how much individual students receive. A deserving student, from a family with no spare cash, might be lucky enough to collect a £5,000 windfall from one institution, while a student from a similar background in another might get much less.

But if universities and colleges want to hand out the cash – and there are some which will be ploughing back a third of their fee income into bursaries – then students are going to grab what's on offer.

13

Grants

The term 'grants' has returned to the language of student finance. But it isn't really the same concept as the grants that funded previous generations of students.

Before the current system of student loans and fees, students were given grants by local education authorities. These were non-repayable, which means there was never any requirement to pay anything back. They were a straightforward gift from the government to help students through university or college. The grants were means-tested, although with a good accountant it always seemed that some of the richest students, as well as the poorest, seemed to end up with full grants.

But this was a system based on only a small minority of young people going into higher education. The current arrangements are based on a model of 'mass participation', in which it's expected that a majority of young people will go into higher education.

The grants that were given to students in the 1970s and before were to cover living costs, such as rent, books, jackets with huge collars and progressive rock LPs. You get the picture, they were to cover whatever students needed to spend. There were no tuition fees to worry about, so none of the complicated loans and repayments existed either. Parents who themselves might have experienced that grant system might now be looking at the promise of grants for today's students, and wondering if the glory days are returning.

The good news is that the new type of grant is also non-repayable. And, like the old grants, they're means-tested in relation to parental income. But it isn't really the case that they will cover living costs because the maximum level of grant from 2006 will be £2,700, which is less than the maximum tuition fee, £3,000. And since most courses are going to cost £3,000, the grant is going to disappear into covering this higher fee.

This shouldn't sound unduly negative, as this grant is an extra amount of money going towards supporting students. But, in practice, it's going to be extra money going in to cover extra money going out. And if you want to buy those progressive rock albums, the money will come out of the student loan, which will have to be paid back.

For students going to university or college in 2005, the 'higher education grant' won't be as high as the £2,700 promised for 2006. Students in 2005–06 can receive up to £1,000 per year, with the amount depending on parents' incomes. It has to be said, however, that these thresholds for the grant, based on the combined incomes of parents, are not exactly generous.

Grants for 2005–06

Where the combined household income is:

- ■ £15,580 or below, students receive £1,000 in grant;
- ■ £16,000, students receive £933;
- ■ £17,000, students receive £774;
- ■ £18,000, students receive £615;
- ■ £19,000, students receive £457;
- ■ £20,000, students receive £298;
- ■ £21,000, students receive £139;
- ■ £21,565, students receive £50.

To apply for a grant contact the local education authority for an application form. Grants are usually paid in three instalments along with the student loan.

Students with children

There are several grants specifically designed for students with dependants that are intended to prevent parenthood being a barrier to going to university or college. The details are tucked away in the small print of the funding proposals but shouldn't disguise the fact that this is quite a valuable subsidy that, for a two-child family, could be worth more than the maximum loan. This is another example of funding being targeted at a perceived area of need, rather than being more broadly applied.

The Childcare Grant

The Childcare Grant provides full-time students with support towards childcare costs, both in term-time and during the holidays. It won't count against other benefit entitlements. It will provide up to 85 per cent of the childcare costs for one child – up to £114.75 per week. For two or more children, there is support for up to 85 per cent of costs – up to £170 per week.

The applications for this support go through the local education authority, and the individuals or organization providing childcare have to confirm how much they are charging. This means that child-care cannot be an informal arrangement with relatives or friends, but has to be with a registered childminder or in an approved childcare setting where there is a verifiable regular expense.

There are no plans for this grant to be changed in 2006.

Parents' Learning Allowance

The childcare subsidy addresses one area of cost for parents, but there are plenty of other expenses. The Parents' Learning Allowance is intended to cover course costs and, as a guide to the likely level of support, the most recent maximum was £1,365 per year. This grant is means-tested against the income of other 'dependants' in the student's household, which can include children or an adult partner.

The thresholds for qualifying for this support, for a couple with two or more children or a lone parent with one child, require the student's dependants to have an annual income of less than £4,095.

For a couple with one child, the dependants' income must be below £3,070. And the earnings limit for a lone parent with more than one child to qualify is £5,120.

Lone Parents' Grant

Just in case this was in danger of becoming simple, there is a complication to the allowances available to lone parents. There is a separate Lone Parents' Grant, which is means-tested, with a maximum value of £1,150 this year. This is also not repayable, but if you receive this particular grant it excludes you from claiming the Parents' Learning Allowance. Also the Lone Parents' Grant can count as income in benefits calculations.

Both the Lone Parents' Grant and the Parents' Learning Allowance are paid at the beginning of each term.

Adult Dependants' Grant

This is intended to help people going to university or college who have an adult who depends on them financially, such as a partner, including same-sex partner, or a relative who might be disabled and unable to support him or herself. This can be worth up to £2,395 per year, depending on means testing, and does not have to be paid back.

Disabled Students' Allowances

For students with disabilities there is a range of special payments available, designed to remove financial barriers that might block access to higher education. It's worth taking time to see what is on offer because there are grants which could be approaching £40,000 over a three-year degree course. Much of the application process for these grants – and the verification for entitlement – will be through the local education authority, so it is also worth making contact to find what support might be available for a particular disability.

These means-tested allowances are available to both full-time and part-time students, with the stipulation that part-time students are not spending more than twice the time expected for an equivalent full-time course. Students can apply at any time for these allowances, even if they have already started a course. And the grants do not have to be paid back.

These allowances can also extend to paying towards the cost of a helper, who might need to provide particular assistance to allow a disabled student to take part in a course. This non-medical helper allowance is up to £11,840 per year, with a reduced amount for part-time students.

Disabilities can also mean extra expenses for course work, such as having to buy special equipment to adapt course materials. There is a grant of £4,680 available for this, but this is given for a whole course rather than as an annual payment. There is also a 'general disabled students' allowance', worth up to a maximum of £1,565 for full-time and £1,170 for part-time students.

For postgraduate students with disabilities, there is a separate non-repayable allowance, worth up to £5,640 per year.

But to claim any of these allowances, there will need to be proof that a student has a specific disability and that extra costs will be incurred. It is not a case of ticking the box and collecting the cash.

This proof is likely to mean a written statement from a doctor or someone else who can provide an appropriate medical opinion on a physical or mental disability. This might be a letter from a psychologist, for instance, or a formal assessment from a suitably qualified professional in a centre attended by the student. The information has to be up to date, and any assessment must be since a student was aged 16 or over – so the authority will not be impressed by a test carried out when the student was in primary school.

The advice from the Department for Education and Skills gives the example of dyslexia. It says that if a student is claiming an allowance for this, it will need proof from someone who works professionally with dyslexics. And if the diagnosis was made before the student was 16, he or she would be expected to have a further test to check the current status of the learning difficulty.

Another reason for contacting the local education authority is to find out exactly what type of proof they expect for different forms of disability and how much detail they will require. The burden of proof for dyslexia is going to be very different from a physical impairment, such as needing to use a wheelchair, or for a mental impairment. And if you send in insufficient information, or the wrong type of supporting evidence, with the application it could mean delays in getting the grant in time.

As well as these allowances from the government, there might be additional support for disabled students from individual local education authorities or from universities and colleges themselves. Again, it's worth inquiring to find out.

Care leavers' grant

There is a grant to help young people who have been in care to pay their way through university or college. This can provide up to £100 per week during the long summer holiday – which means a non-repayable grant worth £1,200. This is intended to help students who are not going to be able to go home to scrounge off their parents for the summer.

But this grant is specifically available to students, aged under 21 when their course began, who were in care before October 2001 when the Children Leaving Care Act was introduced. This legislation was designed to provide a 'pathway plan' for children leaving care – and this includes support for education and accommodation. This means that young people who have been in care since October 2001 should have a personal adviser and access to financial support – and so will not be eligible for the Care leavers' grant.

Travel costs

Most of the travelling undertaken by students will be at their own expense, regardless of how far they have to travel from home. But there are a handful of exceptions where there is some support for extra travel costs. These include a grant for medical and dental students who have to travel for clinical training and assistance for students who have to study abroad as a requirement of their course. If students have to be abroad for more than eight consecutive weeks, there can be a grant to cover the cost of medical insurance.

Whether these costs are 'reasonable' will be decided by the local education authority. If they are accepted the student will be refunded for the cost of travel, minus the first £275, which students will have to pay.

Access to Learning Fund

This is another form of the university or college 'hardship' fund, and is a kind of safety net for students who have pressing financial needs not covered by other grants. It's available through the institution, rather than the local education authority, and is meant to cover financial emergencies or gaps in support for students.

The fund is for both full-time and part-time students and is assessed according to 'individual needs' – but the Department for Education and Skills has a list of priorities for how it should be allocated. This includes students with children, mature students, students from low-income families, disabled students and students in their final year. This gives a flavour of how these funds are intended to be targeted – and that it's not a slush fund to help students who have blown their loans on a particularly good night out. The amount available will vary depending on the university or college and also the specific needs of the applicant – and usually these one-off payments will not have to be paid back.

Teacher training students

In a bid to recruit more students into teaching, there are a number of financial carrots dangled, including grants and subsidies for fees. For students going into a postgraduate teacher training course in 2005 tuition fees do not have to be paid, representing a saving of £1,175. This is in recognition that, after paying tuition fees for three years, students might be reluctant to go into a teacher training course if it meant a fourth year of paying fees. So fees for the postgraduate course (often known as a PGCE) are paid for by the government.

There is also a training bursary for postgraduate teaching students, worth £6,000 for the year (£7,000 for maths and science). This is another recruitment incentive and is intended to stop potential teachers being put off by the prospect of living another year of penury.

There is even more cash on offer if students begin training for a 'shortage subject'. There are some subjects which have a particular shortage of specialist teachers and, as a way of tackling this shortfall, the government has introduced a number of 'golden hellos', where money is available for students training to teach these shortage subjects. These have been worth up to £5,000 to students under 25 years old and £7,500 for mature students, with the list of shortage subjects including science, design and technology, information and communications technology (ICT), maths, music, religious education and modern languages. Applications for these grants are made through the university or college where the teacher training course is held.

Work

It's an ugly four-letter word, but we'd better say it, because it's more likely than ever that students will have part-time jobs when they're at university or college. This shift towards more students working in term time and during the holidays has been one of the biggest changes in student life – and it shows how undeniably hard they are working, combining both studying and earning.

In only four years, the number of students who don't work in either the holidays or during term time has more than halved, from 44 per cent down to a dwindling 20 per cent. And, correspondingly, students' wages have become a growing proportion of their average income. Without making any headlines, money from jobs has become one of the most important forms of student support – not least because it's not means-tested, there are no sliding scales of complicated allowances and no small print. It's a self-service means of funding that is open to anyone.

There have been surveys claiming that about two in five students have jobs in the evening and at weekends. Other reports have put the proportion of working students much higher, including some students' superhuman efforts in maintaining two part-time jobs.

Regular tracking surveys of students suggest that the proportion of students working in term-time jumped sharply upwards a few years ago – possibly reflecting the impact of tuition fees. And it is currently around the 42 per cent mark. When it comes to the long summer holiday, there are estimates that more than half of students take a full-time or part-time job, often stockpiling cash for when they're back at university or college.

Perhaps not surprisingly, fewer students from affluent backgrounds will have jobs in term time. This means that a large majority of students from more modest backgrounds are going to be heading off to work when their lectures finish. Research has also suggested that students living at home with their parents are also much more likely to have term-time jobs.

The reasons for students working are not difficult to imagine. But the top reasons given by students are to help them pay for necessities, to reduce borrowing, to maintain a social life, to buy clothes and to gain skills for life after university or college. And using a part-time job to cut down on borrowing is a sound investment, as it reduces the debt that will be waiting to be paid off after graduation.

Current average student earnings are claimed by the Unite/Mori survey to be £86 per week, which would represent £2,580 per year and £7,740 during a three-year course. And that's not taking into account any work during the long summer holiday. But earnings will depend on the local jobs market – and a survey in the north-west of England claimed that most students were earning average pay of £4.50 per hour or less. Employment agencies that are used by students say that the type of jobs they might carry out, such as clerical work and in call centres, might pay about £6 or £7 per hour, which would bring in £600 or £700 per term for a student working 10 hours per week.

How many hours students are currently working each week during term time is not really certain. There are universities and colleges that advise that students should not work more than 10 hours a week, and there are others that set a higher recommended limit of 15 hours a week. An annual survey has claimed an average of 14 hours worked each week by students, but there are reports that students are putting in as many as 30 hours a week, on top of their course work.

Inevitably there are difficulties balancing these two commitments – and surveys have found students reporting that their studies have been adversely affected by their part-time jobs. Although they might not miss lectures and seminars, students report problems with tiredness, stress, and pressure on study time.

If you're looking for a job, many universities and colleges provide information and contacts for work. And, in fact, higher education institutions are often a source of work themselves. But there is no reason why students shouldn't also use the Job Centre Plus service, which can give details of part-time work, either over the phone or using a touch-screen system. There are also employment agencies, which will charge for their services, and classified adverts in newspapers.

Students are not limited to archetypal jobs such as bar work or waiting on tables in restaurants. As an example of the types of jobs undertaken by students, one university lists vacancies in administration, computer-based work, telemarketing, promotions, market research, call centres, translation, retail and driving. The largest single area of employment appears to be in retail. Shops are staying open longer hours and there is more demand for flexible, part-time workers, and the checkouts of all-night supermarkets can provide the kind of night life that students might not have expected. Although it might be tempting to take on lots of shifts, however, there's no point getting a few more quid if it ruins the chance of studying. If you burn yourself out with overwork, it's going to defeat the object of going to university or college.

Even though students are only part-time and temporary workers, there is no reason why they should be exploited. And rules such as the minimum wage apply to students as much as to anyone else. The current minimum for 18- to 21-year-olds is £4.10 per hour, and for workers over 21 the legal minimum is £4.85. In October 2005 the minimum wage for younger workers will rise to £4.25, and above that age workers must be paid £5.05 per hour. The following year, in October 2006, these rates should rise to £4.45 per hour for younger workers and £5.35 for older workers. The exception to this is students on course-related work placement schemes, who are not entitled to the minimum wage.

There are also rights that all employers have to respect, such as not discriminating against staff on the grounds of race, sex or disability. After a month in a job, an employer has to give at least a week's notice of dismissal. And after a year, even if someone is working part-time, they are entitled to claim for unfair dismissal.

Student workers should also know their rights about rests and breaks between shifts. If the working day is six hours, there is an entitlement to a 20-minute break. And there must be at least an 11-hour gap between ending one shift and starting the next.

Even though someone has to have a job for a year before they can appeal against unfair dismissal, there are rules that prevent certain types of dismissal whenever it happens. An employer can't sack someone because she is pregnant or because he or she refuses to carry out a dangerous task. And a worker cannot be sacked for asserting the right to be paid the minimum wage.

Safety at work is very important, even if you're only there for a few hours a week. It might not seem like a big issue, but workers who are unfamiliar with machinery or equipment can be even more vulnerable to accidents. There have been grim cases of students taking temporary jobs that have ended in serious accidents.

Safety advice from the trade unions warns that students who are not aware of their rights have been forced into very dangerous working conditions. And employees have a right to refuse to carry out a task if there is an 'imminent and serious danger'.

When it comes to paying income tax, students are in the same position as any other worker. But unless they have a particularly lucrative summer job, they should be able to stay within the 'personal allowance' of what someone can earn before they pay tax. At present the allowance is £4,745 per year and, as long as students earn less than that amount, they won't have to pay income tax.

It is not all doom and gloom for student workers. Aside from the social benefits of work, such as meeting people, having a term-time job is reported by many students to be a useful way of gaining skills that will later be useful in full-time jobs. In a survey, almost three-quarters of students with jobs claimed that they felt they had benefited from the experience.

15

Sponsorship

As well as financial support from the government, parents and the universities and colleges, another occasional source of funding for students is sponsorship. This doesn't mean that you'll be wearing the logo of a major telecommunications company for three years, or be forced to use their advertising slogans at the beginning of your conversations. Instead, it is a kind of individualized donation made by organizations that have money available for students – usually for no more than a handful each year.

This donation might be from a business, a charity, an educational trust or some philanthropist who has bequeathed some cash to needy students. The availability will depend very much on the course you're doing and how it fits in with the intentions of whoever is supplying the sponsorship. But it's certainly worth making inquiries.

Big companies often have some funding for deserving students in their particular field. Students might be considered deserving because they're hugely talented, or else it might be because they're broke. These types of sponsorship arrangements are entirely at the discretion of the donor and there's no set pattern.

Some subject areas seem to be more likely to attract sponsorship, such as engineering and science. For example, the oil and petrochemical industry might support chemistry and physics students. But sponsorship isn't always from technology-heavy industry. The high street retailers, Marks and Spencer, have a scheme for disadvantaged students.

These sponsorships can be a form of early recruitment, establishing a relationship with students that organizations might want to employ.

Or else it can be a case of wanting to encourage a wider pool of people who are studying a subject that is relevant to their business. Sponsorship deals with companies can involve some kind of work placement or holiday job, which will provide useful experience as well as the tempting prospect of a few quid in extra support. This might be worth somewhere in the region of £1,000 for a year. But a work placement year will draw much more cash and will be more like a proper salary. Such schemes might only be available to final year students, so don't assume that you have to put in for such funding at the outset of a degree course.

There can be arrangements between sponsors and individual universities and colleges. Or else universities and colleges might have access to legacies which will support a couple of worthy cases each year.

It's not a form of funding on which you can depend, but it's worth looking into whether your subject or higher education institution makes you eligible to apply for support. This will take a little research, because sponsorship is not in any kind of centralized system but is available according to the whims of the donor.

There are a few useful starting points. Universities and colleges and their student unions will have information about support that is specific to the institution. And there are directories of sponsors that you might be able to get through the university or college library, such as the *Educational Grants Directory*, published by the Directory of Social Change; *Sponsorship and Funding Directory*, published by Hobsons; and *Engineering Opportunities for Students and Graduates*, published by the Institution of Mechanical Engineers.

Even though it might seem hit and miss, using the internet is a way of searching for support in your area of study. Corporate websites might have information about scholarships and awards, or professional bodies and trade associations might have links to sources of funding.

16

Part-time students

Students who are studying part time have often been overlooked in all the arguments about funding. They have been part of the jigsaw that has never quite fitted, as the system has really been shaped around school-leavers going into full-time degree courses.

But this is a fast-growing section of the student population, as more people decide to go back to university or college. According to Universities UK, since the mid-1990s the number of part-time students has risen by 75 per cent. And in 11 universities, part-time students are now in the majority. It's estimated that there are half a million part-time students.

Who are these part-time students? A survey carried out for the Department for Education and Skills found that the average part-time student is aged 37, a woman and with a full-time job. And it suggests a pattern of people who, because of work and family commitments, want to study in a more flexible way. It can include people who missed out on university or college when they were younger, or it might be people working full time who are studying job-related courses that will help them with their careers.

Even though there is financial support available for part-time students, the make-up of the part-time student population suggests that most of them will be relying on their own resources or else getting funding from their employers. Almost two-thirds of part-time students are in full-time jobs and another 18 per cent are working part time, so many of these students will be paying their own way through university or college. Only one in 20 part-time students is otherwise unemployed. More than a third of part-time students get all their fees paid by an employer – and almost two-thirds of those in work get help from their employers.

This year will see the introduction of more extensive financial support. Students in England and Wales, who are following a part-time course that is 50–59 per cent or more of a full-time course, can apply for a grant towards tuition fees of £590. For students who are studying more 'intensively', 60–74 per cent of a full-time degree course, there is a fee grant of £710, and for students on courses equivalent to 75 per cent of a full-time course there is a fee grant of £885.

Part-time tuition fees typically range between £400 and £1,000 per year, with universities and colleges setting their own levels for different courses. The biggest differences in price are not between universities and colleges but between subjects and the intensity of study. What will happen to part-time tuition fees from 2006 remains unclear, however, as there is no provision for the deferred repayment that will come with higher fees for full-time students.

There is also a grant of up to £250 towards the costs of the course, such as books and travel. This is means-tested support, against students' income if they're working, or against their partner's income. The income threshold to qualify for the full support is £14,970 or less. The maximum income level for claiming some support is £22,000.

The calculations for income are also slightly more generous in that £2,000 of income can be discounted if a part-time student has one child – and £1,000 each for other dependent children. Students with partners can also discount £2,000 from their income. This means that a married part-time student with two children could have a household income of £19,970 and still qualify for the full amount of support.

These allowances will be available to existing as well as to new part-time students. Support can last up to eight years and there is no age limit, but students who already have a degree are usually excluded from this support.

Applications for this funding should be made through your local education authority or by calling a central student support information number, 0800 731 9133. The application form has to be taken to your college for confirmation that you are a part-time student, that you are studying 50 per cent of a full-time course and of how much is paid in fees. This form should then be sent to your local education authority, or Open University students should send the form to the Open University (01908 653411).

Part-time students can also put in for support from the Access to Learning Fund (details in the Grants section, Chapter 13). This might be able to assist with specific costs such as childcare. If appropriate, the Disabled Students' Allowances are available to part-time students.

Another option is a career development loan, which can be between £300 and £8,000, and usually covers two years of work-related education. Students do not pay any interest while they're studying, but once they have finished they have to take responsibility for repaying the loan and any interest charges. Information is available from 0800 585505.

17

Healthcare students

There is a separate funding system for 'healthcare' students which covers a range of people training for jobs within the health services. It also covers students whose courses are much longer than the usual three-year degree, so who will need more financial support. Doctors and dentists, for instance, are treated as ordinary students for the first three years. But when it comes to the fourth year and beyond, they enter the category of healthcare students.

NHS bursaries

These are grants from the health service for students studying a wide range of health-related courses. As well as medical and dentistry students this includes nurses, midwives, chiropodists, occupational therapists, physiotherapists, speech therapists, dental hygienists and audiologists. The bursaries are intended to help students with living costs and are usually paid in monthly instalments directly into the student's bank account. The full amount is £2,768 per year in London, £2,253 outside London and £1,843 for students living at home.

For nursing and midwifery students the NHS bursaries are not means-tested. They provide a 'flat basic maintenance grant' and do not require any parental contribution. For other degree level and postgraduate courses the bursaries are means-tested against the earnings of the students and their parents.

Doctors and dentists

Medical and dental students will spend the first four years of their courses having the same support as other students in terms of loans, grants and fees. But in the fifth year and beyond students do not have tuition fees to pay. And they will be able to apply for the non-repayable NHS bursaries. They will also be able to apply for loans.

For students on accelerated four-year graduate medicine degrees, bursaries, loans and fee assistance are available from the second year of the course.

Childcare allowance

This provides up to 85 per cent of the cost of childcare for students who have children. There is an upper limit of about £115 per week for one child and £170 per week for two children. The single parent addition also provides £1,153 per year.

Extra weeks allowance

Healthcare students often have longer terms than the standard degree and there are extra allowances for extra weeks. In London there is a rate of £96 per week extra, and outside London £75 per week.

Older students' allowance

This offers extra support for mature students. Anyone who is over 25 will receive £397 extra, and there are higher payments for 25- to 29-year-olds, who receive £1,348.

Two homes and placement costs

If the training means a student has to live away from home, there is a grant of £813 to cover extra accommodation costs. There is also a travel allowance to cover the costs of getting to and from his or her placement.

Student loans

Healthcare students can sometimes claim a student loan to help cover living costs, because the NHS bursary is unlikely to be enough on its own. Details about whether a particular student will be able to claim a loan will be available from his or her local education authority. For healthcare students living in London the loan, at current rates, can be up to £2,480; outside London it is £2,005.

Applying for NHS grants

When students are offered an NHS-funded place, the NHS Student Grants Unit should send them an application form for financial support.

NHS Grants Unit, 22 Plymouth Road, Blackpool FY3 7JS. Tel: 01253 655655. Website: www.nhspa.gov.uk.

Or contact the NHS Careers Helpline: 0845 6060655, www.nhs.uk/careers.

18

Independent students

Not all students will fit into the pattern of teenagers leaving their family home to go to university or college, supported by the good wishes and wallet-power of their parents. Students who are no longer considered to be dependants of their parents are given 'independent' status, which means that their parents' income is not taken into account when assessing the amount of financial support they will receive.

This category includes what used to be known as 'mature students', who are returning to studying after working or having children. These students might have their own home and the support of a working partner, but they will still have costs such as fees and course materials, which from 2006 will represent a considerable outlay and might require access to a student loan.

The chapter on how much university or college costs looks in more detail at what has to be paid, in terms of covering what would have been the parental contribution in addition to the loan. Also, many mature students with family commitments are studying part time, so check the chapter on what support is available for part-time students.

In terms of receiving financial assistance, the same amounts are due to full-time independent students as to anyone else. So the loans, grants and bursaries are available to the same level as they are to other students.

To be defined as an independent student you must be either aged 25 or over, be married when the course starts or have supported yourself independently for three years. This category also includes students whose parents have died, or where contact with parents has seriously broken down.

Because this arrangement means that parents will not be making contributions there will be a requirement for evidence of such break-downs in relationships. This might be a letter from a social worker, school or a doctor, giving evidence that there is a permanent estrangement. This independent status is also applied if making contact with the parent could put the student at some kind of risk.

Such tight regulations might sound petty, but presumably they are designed to stop families inventing a big bust-up to dodge the expected parental payments towards the cost of university or college. So the regulations rule out simply having stopped living at home as sufficient proof of such a complete end of a relationship and parental responsibility.

This can be difficult for students who appear to be from well-off families, but where the relationship is so dysfunctional that they're not getting any help. If parents are separating and their finances are in an acrimonious mess, it can be the student who can get left in the lurch. Student unions have stories of young people from wealthy families who do not get what they should from their families – but who do not qualify for the extra loan money available to 'poorer' students.

Apart from not means-testing their parents, other arrangements are going to be similar, so independent students will still face the same level of tuition fees and other costs. But in the case of a financial emergency, it is worth contacting the university or college and student welfare services, because there are safety-net funds available under schemes such as the Access to Learning Fund.

Calling all Scottish students studying in the UK

If you are a Scottish student on a higher education course (HNC level and above) you may be eligible for:

- help with tuition fees; **££££**
- living costs (student loan and a bursary);
- supplementary grants.

How do I do this?

You can apply to The Student Awards Agency for Scotland (SAAS) for help to do your course. SAAS is part of the Scottish Executive and provides financial support to eligible Scottish domiciled students on courses of higher education.

Contacting SAAS

Visit their website at **www.saas.gov.uk**

E-mail them at saas.geu@scotland.gsi.gov.uk

Phone them on **0845 111 1711**

Write to them at:
The Student Awards Agency for Scotland
Gyleview House
3 Redheughs Rigg
Edinburgh
EH12 9HH

19

Scotland

Tuition fees

The biggest difference between students in England and in Scotland is that Scottish students, regardless of their family income, do not have to pay tuition fees. Instead there is a system of repayment after graduation, called the 'graduate endowment'.

In terms of support, this means that Scottish students at Scottish universities and colleges get their £1,175 fees paid for them by the Student Awards Agency for Scotland. Whether a fee exists if you don't have to pay it is something of a philosophical question (or a political fudge), but in terms of pounds and pence the students don't have to hand over the cash. While the English system is about to experiment with a market in variable fees, the Scottish system seems to be sticking with keeping fees out of the equation.

Means-testing

The other big difference for financial support is that the Scottish system is more directly structured around helping students from lower-income families. While under the English system, only a quarter of the student loan depends on the income of the student's family, under the Scottish system about four-fifths of the loan is means-tested.

Even if students in Scotland do not have to worry about fees, they will still need this student loan to pay for the living costs of rent, bills and food. And, as elsewhere in the UK, this is administered by the Student Loans Company.

The total package of bursaries and loans could see a student from a low-income family receiving £4,740 per year in support, plus the £1,175 for tuition fees.

Bursaries

Scotland has its own set of non-repayable grants, for Scottish students at Scottish universities and colleges, which are aimed at helping students from low-income families.

There is a means-tested Young Students' Bursary worth up to £2,395, which will provide help with living costs and is available for students from families with an income of £17,500 or below. There is some bursary available for students from families earning up to £31,000.

The availability of the Young Students' Bursary is:

■ family income of £17,500, £2,395 bursary;
■ family income of £18,000, £2,307 bursary;
■ family income of £20,000, £1,956 bursary;
■ family income of £22,000, £1,605 bursary;
■ family income of £24,000, £1,254 bursary;
■ family income of £26,000, £903 bursary;
■ amily income of £28,000, £552 bursary;
■ family income of £30,000, £202 bursary;
■ family income of £31,000, £26 bursary;
■ family income of £32,000, £0 bursary.

To be a 'young' person in this context means being aged 25 or under, unmarried and not having supported yourself for three years since leaving school. In effect, what this really means is that this bursary is mostly going to go to students who have just left school or taken a year out, but who are still part of their parental family.

Receiving this bursary will have a knock-on effect for student loans. Any amount received from the bursary will be deducted from the money available in the student loan. The downside of this is that the bursary isn't going to be in addition to the loan. But the upside is that it lowers the amount of loan to be repaid, as a chunk of the loan will now be this non-repayable bursary.

There is also a Mature Students' Bursary Fund, but the universities and colleges, who decide about who should qualify, allocate this. Applications are made directly to the institution.

Student loans

The backbone of the student finance system, which will cover the day-to-day living costs, is the student loan. After students have graduated and are working, they pay the money back to the Student Loans Company.

Even though no government would ever say that this is a type of tax, the repayments are taken at source out of monthly pay, alongside income tax and National Insurance. And like tax and National Insurance, payments are triggered once you go above a certain level of income, which for student loans is £15,000 per year.

Even though this is a loan, and so will have to be repaid, the student loan is not like a commercial loan, where the bank is taking its own slice in interest charges. The repayments will include a slight increase to match inflation, but there is no interest charge, so this is effectively a cost-free advance.

Because of this, there is a limit on how much of this interest-free credit is available – with each student's allocation depending on the means-testing of their family income. Richer families are deemed to need less of this interest-free loan than poor families, with the calculations assuming that richer families will give their children more support.

Whether these richer families really do hand over the cash is another matter, but it is the wealth of students and their families that will determine the size of their loan.

The figures

For Scottish students who are living away from home when they're at a Scottish university or college the maximum loan is £4,195 per year, of which £3,365 is means-tested. In the student's final year, this is reduced to £3,645 per year, of which £2,935 will be means-tested.

For Scottish students who are living at home when they're at a Scottish university or college the maximum loan is £3,320, of which £2,775 is means-tested. In the student's final year this is reduced to £2,900, of which £2,460 will be means-tested.

These figures show the extent to which the loan will depend on the income of the students or their parents. With a family income of below £22,010, students will receive the full loan. But once the combined parental income starts getting above £50,000, then the student is going to get very little support.

And for those assessed as being too rich to get any of the means-tested loan there is only a meagre £830 per year. So these students will depend heavily on their parents.

What is a Scottish student?

For the purposes of getting financial support for students, the definition of being Scottish is quite specific. This isn't a question of national identity or family background so much as a question of where you usually live. And feeling that you're really Scottish, even though you've lived all your life in north London, won't be enough.

First of all, the student needs to have been resident in the UK for three years before the course begins. And non-UK nationals will also have been 'settled' in the country, as defined by the Home Office.

And the next criteria is that the student is ordinarily resident in Scotland, with this residency defined as 'habitual and normal residence in one place'. This means Scotland being the place where someone lives for 'year after year' apart from 'temporary or occasional absences'. And it rejects any attempt at opportunistic attempts to be Scottish.

'Living here totally or mainly for the purpose of receiving full-time education does not count as being ordinarily resident', says the awards agency.

Scottish students outside Scotland

Scottish students outside Scotland are able to apply for an income-assessed contribution to tuition fees – which means they might get help for all or some of the £1,175 fee charged in English universities and colleges. There is a separate Young Students' Outside Scotland bursary, which offers an extra £530 to students from low-income families in addition to the loan.

Scottish students going to study in English universities or colleges will also be able to apply for a loan to help with living costs. The maximum loan amounts will be the same – £4,195 for students outside London, £5,175 for students in London.

But a larger amount of the loan will not be income assessed. For Scottish students in London universities and colleges the minimum, non-assessed element of the loan is £2,170, and outside London the non-assessed amount is £2,010 (compared to £830 for a Scottish student in Scotland).

Additional loan

This support is, as you might have guessed, an additional loan. It's a means-tested amount, up to a maximum of £545, which will provide a top-up to the loan for students from a fairly narrowly targeted range of low-income families.

The family income threshold to get the full £530 is £16,590 or under. Smaller amounts of additional loan are available up to an income of £19,730.

Dependants' Grant

There is a means-tested, non-repayable grant of up to £2,395 available for students who have a married dependent partner. For eligibility contact the Student Awards Agency for Scotland.

Lone Parents' Grant

Extra support for lone parents with dependent children is available as a grant of up to £1,180. For parents receiving this grant there is support available for childcare, worth up £1,100. This has to be in a formal setting, such as with a registered childminder or in a nursery. This grant would be paid each term along with the Lone Parents' Grant.

Applying for support

The advice is to apply early to make sure that any financial support for which you might be eligible is paid on time. This would be as soon as a student has a conditional (or unconditional) offer of a place.

For students going to university or college for the first time in 2005, you can apply online for support for fees and living costs, using the Student Awards Agency for Scotland website (www.saas.gov.uk). Students who do not want to apply online can still download the application forms directly from the same website. These forms are available for undergraduates, postgraduates, nursing and midwifery and part-time and distance learning students.

Applicants will then be told by the agency how much support they will be receiving, and the information will be passed to the Student Loans Company – who will pay the loan directly to the student's bank account when the course begins. Support for fees will be paid directly to the student's higher education institution – and any bursary will be sent to the student's bank account or to the institution for collection.

20

Wales

The big increase in tuition fees already announced for English universities and colleges in 2006 is not going to happen in Wales – or at least it's not going to happen for the next couple of years. So the new grants being made available for students in Wales will not be about offsetting a hike in fees.

Responsibility for decisions about tuition fees has been devolved to the National Assembly – and the assembly has said that the 'variable' fee system being introduced in England will not be brought to Wales in the duration of the current assembly. This means that the variable fees (which in England allows universities and colleges to decide how much they're going to charge up to £3,000 per year) will not be in Wales until at least 2007. And, at the time of writing, it remains to be decided how the fees system will operate from 2007–08.

But even if there isn't a variable fee for 2006, there will still be a fixed fee, to be decided by the National Assembly. And, like the system to be introduced in England, repayments of fees will be after graduation.

Assembly Learning Grant

The Welsh Assembly has been providing its own grant to 'provide extra money for students who might otherwise experience financial difficulty'. This grant targets money at low-income families, defined for 2004–05 as those students whose families earn less than £15,721 per year.

The maximum that full-time higher education students can claim is £1,500, which is available to families with an income of up to £5,240. For those earning up to £10,470, £750 in grant is available and for those earning up to £15,720, there is £450 per year.

This is a non-repayable grant given in addition to student loans and is intended to help with living costs. Applications for the grant are made through the local education authority.

Higher Education Grant

The Assembly Learning Grant overlaps with the Higher Education Grant that is being introduced, which has a value of up to £1,000. Students can't have both, so if you are given the maximum Higher Education Grant, but would have also qualified for the maximum Assembly Learning Grant, the extra £500 can be added as a 'top-up'.

Students who have already started at university or college and have been receiving an Assembly Learning Grant will continue to do so.

When the new tuition fee system is introduced in England in 2006, there is going to be a means-tested grant to cover most of the fees for less well-off students. And in Wales the same amount of money is going to be given as a grant, which will incorporate the current Assembly Learning Grant. Whatever this incoming grant is called, it will be worth £2,700 per year.

For Welsh students at English universities and colleges, this £2,700 is likely to be spent on paying the tuition fees, which will be up to £3,000.

Student loans

While the grants will provide a little more cash for students from low-income families, the basic support for students' living costs will come from the student loan. This interest-free loan, administered by the Student Loans Company, will begin to be repaid once a student has graduated and is earning more than £15,000 per year.

The maximum that a student can borrow, using figures from 2004 as a guide, is £5,050 for a student attending a higher education institution in London. Outside of London, the maximum is £4,095, and for students living with their parents, the maximum is £3,240. These figures are the maximum that the Student Loans Company will lend – with the largest loans being made available to students from the families with the lowest incomes.

The idea is that the government will provide the full loan to those students whose families cannot afford to make a contribution. And, conversely, students from the richest families will receive the smallest loans, on the grounds that the parents can shoulder a larger share of the burden.

But, despite this means-tested element of the loan, the majority of the loan amount is available to everyone – with only about a quarter of the full loan amount being dependent on income assessment. This means that all Welsh students at Welsh universities and colleges will receive at least £3,071 in loans – and up to an additional £1,024 depending on family income. The higher the family income, the lower the amount of means-tested loan available – with the parental contribution expected to make up the difference, up to this maximum of £1,024.

The section on 'How much will it cost?' (Part Three) gives a full breakdown of what parents will be expected to pay and how repayments for loans are worked out. But, in general, once a student has graduated and is earning the equivalent of £15,000 per year, then 9 per cent of everything earned above this level will go towards paying off the loan. As an example, the Learning Wales information service says students earning £18,000 will be repaying £5.19 per week.

21

Northern Ireland

The different student finance systems now evolving in Scotland and Wales reflect the way in which devolved governments are choosing their own paths for supporting students through university or college. In Northern Ireland, the future shape of student finance will be linked to the political developments in the way Northern Ireland is governed. But, at the time of writing, with devolution on hold, student support in Northern Ireland, for those starting in 2005, is broadly similar to the English system.

Student loans

Students will for the most part depend on the interest-free student loans for their living expenses, such as accommodation and food. These are provided through the Student Loans Company and are repaid in instalments after students have graduated and are working.

The student loan available is the same as in the English system, with a maximum of £5,050 for students at a London institution, £4,095 for students at universities and colleges outside London and £3,240 for students living at home.

About three-quarters of this will be available to all students, regardless of their family's income. But £1,354 of the loan is means-tested – and the wealthier the family, the less interest-free loan is made available. And the parental contribution is meant to make up the difference.

This means that the maximum amount of the loan that a parent will be expected to contribute is £1,354 per year. And the least a student (outside London) will receive as a loan is £2,741 per year. But the parent, depending on the means test, can also be liable to contribute towards tuition fees.

Tuition fees

The tuition fees for 2005 are the same as in the English model, to be paid up front, at a level of £1,175. And there is also the same means-tested support to cover all or some of the cost of the fees.

But there is a slightly more generous upper income threshold than in England, as families in Northern Ireland need to earn an income of £35,287 before their student offspring have to pay the full tuition fee. Students from families earning less than £21,475 won't pay any fees, and anything between £21,475 and £35,287 will mean paying part of the fee.

There is a difference for Northern Irish students who attend university or college in the Irish Republic – their tuition fees are paid for by the Irish government. And the charges for registration, exam fees and student services for universities and colleges in the Irish Republic will be paid for by the student's education and library board.

Grants

There is a Higher Education Bursary aimed at students from low-income families. These non-repayable awards are worth up to £2,000 and are to help with living costs. To qualify for the full amount, the student's family must have an income less than £10,250. Students whose parents earn up to £20,500 will qualify for some lower level of support. For example, a student whose parents have an income of £15,000 to £16,000 will receive a £900 bursary.

Other support

Students in Northern Ireland, where eligible, can also claim support from the Childcare Grant, Parents' Learning Allowance, Lone Parent

Grant, Adult Dependants' Grant and Disabled Students' Allowance. Details of all these awards are given in the section on Grants (Chapter 13).

Applications for support are processed by the education and library boards.

22

Overseas students

There are projections that the number of overseas students at UK universities and colleges could treble in the next couple of decades, with the global market in international education expanding rapidly. This will be good news for the institutions, because overseas students (which usually means anyone from outside the UK or European Union) provide a higher level of fee income than their UK counterparts. And, as higher education institutions continue their unending battle to balance their finances, there has been talk that they might deliberately increasing the proportion of overseas students on courses to generate more cash to support the places for home-grown students.

For the overseas students themselves, who are paying the higher fees, there are some limited grants that are available specifically for them. But it won't usually be possible for overseas students to claim the type of support available to UK students in terms of grants and loans. In practice, many overseas students can only afford to study in the UK because they are getting funding from their own governments or employers – or else because they're just plain rich. Fees and basic living costs for an overseas science student could easily be about £20,000 a year.

There are some limited exceptions to how the 'overseas' status is interpreted. If students can show they have been resident for three years in the UK (not as a student) they might be able to pay the lower rate of tuition fee as paid by UK students.

And the fairly obvious advice dished out to overseas students by the higher education authorities is not to turn up in the UK without any way of financially supporting themselves. Apart from anything else, if a student can't show any evidence of financial support, there's a chance they'll be turned back at the immigration desk.

However, there are some scholarships and grants available from the UK – and application should be made long before the course begins so that the student knows what, if any, extra support is available.

As you will see from the list below there are a range of grants – but they are narrowly targeted and usually only cover part of the costs. They are mostly for postgraduates and do not offer a general maintenance grant for overseas undergraduates. A useful starting point for information is the British Council (www.britishcouncil.org), which acts as a kind of cultural and educational embassy network. If the overseas student has a British Council office in their own country, it is worth contacting them for information about studying in the UK and about financial support.

An even more useful tool for looking for support is the internet, as much of the information and advice is on the websites of the various awarding organizations. And, if what you want to know isn't there, you can always e-mail or get phone numbers for more information.

Scholarships

Among the scholarship schemes are:

British Chevening Scholarships

These are funded by the Foreign Office (www.fco.gov.uk) and provide grants for postgraduate students who show the potential to be 'decision-makers' in their own country. It's a kind of 'make friends and influence people' concept, targeted at students from countries with which 'the UK's economic relations are expected to develop'.

Selection of students is made through local British Embassies and British Council offices. United States students are excluded from applying.

Commonwealth Scholarship and Fellowship Plan

Funded by the Department for International Development (www.dfid.gov.uk) and the Foreign Office, these grants are for students from Commonwealth countries, usually for postgraduate courses. They provide help with travel, fees and living expenses and can include support for a spouse.

Applications are through the Commonwealth Scholarship Agency (contact details from www.thecommonwealth.org) in the student's own country.

The DFID Shared Scholarship Scheme

This is another scholarship aimed at academically able students, under the age of 35, from developing countries in the Commonwealth. Funded by the Department for International Development, it's intended to train students in subjects that will help the development of their countries when they return.

Applicants need to be fluent English speakers, and cannot be employees of their own government or international organizations.

The UK universities taking part in this scheme vary from year to year. Details are available from the local British Council, the Department for International Development or the Association of Commonwealth Universities (www.acu.ac.uk).

Overseas Research Students Awards Scheme

This is for postgraduate research students, is awarded on merit, and will cover the difference between the tuition fees paid by UK students and by overseas students. It does not provide help with living costs, so anyone applying for this award will still need to have money to pay for themselves.

Applications for this award are made through the university where the overseas student will be studying.

Royal Society Fellowships

These are designed to help post-doctoral scientists who are carrying out research in the UK. Further information is available from www.royalsociety.org.

British Marshall Scholarships

These are for young graduates from the United States who want to study at a UK university. They provide support for travel, tuition fees and living costs, and are initially made for two years. Awards are made on a competitive basis.

Further information can be obtained from the British Council or directly from www.marshallscholarship.org.

Fulbright Scholarships

These are jointly funded by the UK and US governments and are aimed at US graduates of all ages studying at UK universities. They provide support for nine months for travel, living costs and fees, and are awarded on a competitive basis.

There are three-month awards available for lecturers or advanced research students, research librarians and academic administrators. Further information is available from www.fulbright.co.uk.

Other support programmes

There are other potential sources of support for overseas students. The EU encourages foreign exchanges between universities in member countries, under schemes such as Socrates and Leonardo. Information about this will be available in the student's own university or country.

And there might be specific grants available from international agencies, development organizations, or from universities themselves – but it's a case of finding such opportunities on an individual basis.

Connect Youth

Giving young people international experiences

Would you like to travel abroad and meet young people from other parts of the world?

Connect Youth offers programmes that give young people an international experience. Every year we send and receive over twenty thousand young people on programmes ranging from group youth exchanges to individual voluntary service. We believe that bringing young people together not only provides them with the opportunity to experience and appreciate new cultures but also teaches them more about themselves.

For groups of young people between 15 and 25 years, we offer funding for:

- _travelling abroad, meeting groups of young people from different countries, taking up activities of mutual interest and host groups from abroad in return_

- _creating, devising and managing projects within the local community. Past projects have covered various themes from youth newspapers to arts festivals and trading enterprises._

For individual young people we offer:

- _the European Voluntary Service, which allows individual young people aged 18 to 25 to act as volunteers abroad, for a period up to a year. They can work in a variety of settings including the care sector, with children, people with disability, or with the elderly_

- _you could also join summer camps in Israel, the West Bank or Macedonia, and teach English to young children._

Our programmes are open to all British young people; there are no entry qualifications to take part. You can choose from over forty countries from Europe and beyond. All activities are supported by funding from the European Commission (European YOUTH Programme), Foreign and Commonwealth Office and the Department for Education and Skills.

For more information, contact
Connect Youth
British Council
10 Spring Gardens
London SW1A 2BN
Tel 020 7389 4030, Fax 020 7389 4033
Email connectyouth.enquiries@britishcouncil.org
www.connectyouthinternational.com

Education and Culture

The European YOUTH Programme

Launched over ten years ago, the European Community's Co-operation Policy in the youth field has stimulated the development of national and local initiatives involving young people, aimed particularly at the less advantaged. It has also offered an opportunity for opening up contact to other countries.

Connect Youth, a department of the British Council, is the official National Agency for the European Youth Programme. It helps to implement, administrate and improve all the activities that can be carried out under the umbrella of the European YOUTH Programme. These activities include: Youth Exchanges, European Voluntary Service, Youth Initiatives and Training Opportunities.

The Programme aims to help young people:
– Acquire knowledge, skills and competencies, and recognise their value
– Become more integrated into society at large
– Gain greater access, in particular, for those living in difficult circumstances, or with some form of disability while helping to eliminate all forms of discrimination
– Encourage active participation with all groups in society (i.e. citizenship)
– Give free expression to their sense of solidarity in Europe and the wider world
– Play an active role in the construction of Europe and promote a better understanding of the diversity of our common European culture.

How does the YOUTH Programme relate to other EU programmes?
The YOUTH Programme is not an isolated European Community initiative. Together with Socrates and Leonardo da Vinci, it is one of several programmes aimed at creating a European space for education – both formal and non-formal – and vocational training.

How is the YOUTH Programme structured?
Building on the experience of both the Youth for Europe and the European Voluntary Service programmes, the YOUTH Programme works through the following kind of projects.

Youth for Europe by promoting and financing group exchanges Volunteering with its European Voluntary Service Young people's own initiatives through Youth Initiatives Maintaining and improving the quality of the projects with training opportunities for those already involved in the Programme Measures.

The National Agencies
Each National Agency acts as a link between the European Commission and support projects at national, regional and local level. Connect Youth,

through its twelve UK committees, helps to develop and manage the programme. They also play an important role in the partner-finding process by providing interested youth with information and links to other countries.

Which countries are eligible to participate?

There are thirty-one eligible countries. These are divide into three groups:

EU countries

Austria, Belgium, Cyprus, Czech Republic, Denmark, Estonia, Finland, France, Germany, Greece, Hungary, Ireland, Italy, Latvia, Lithuania, Luxembourg, Malta, Netherlands, Poland, Portugal, Slovak Republic, Slovenia, Spain, Sweden and United Kingdom

Countries of the European Economic Area

Iceland, Liechtenstein and Norway

EU pre accession countries

Bulgaria, Romania and Turkey

Are other countries involved?

For the purpose of the YOUTH Programme, other countries are referred to as 'third countries'.

Youth exchange activities with third countries must always involve at least two EU Member States and two countries from one of the following four groups.

Mediterranean partner countries

Algeria, Egypt, Israel, Jordan, Lebanon, Morocco, Turkey, Ukraine

Eastern Europe and Caucasus

Armenia, Azerbaijan, Belarus, Georgia, Syria, Moldova, Tunisia, Russia West Bank and Gaza Strip, South-east Europe, Albania, Bosnia and Herzegovina, Macedonia, Croatia, Serbia and Montenegro, (including UNMIK AP Kosovo)

Latin America

Argentina, Bolivia Brazil, Chile, Colombia, Costa Rica, Cuba, Ecuador, Guatemala, Honduras, México, Nicaragua, Panamá, Paraguay, Perú, El Salvador, Uruguay and Venezuela

Special conditions applying to the Mediterranean countries

Other countries are included on a case-by-case basis, according to current political priorities of the European Commission.

British government funds are available to support bilateral exchange projects with China, Japan, Russia, Ukraine, Israel, Palestinian Territories and USA.

So whether you want to create an exchange with a youth group, do voluntary work, or design a project that changes your own community, then Connect Youth can help.

Looking for financial support?

Now there is a new and easy **online** service.

Here you can **apply** for student financial support.

You can **maintain** your account updating personal information, including your telephone number, address and bank account details, even if you have not actually applied on line.

Your questions can be **answered** and you will be able to **view** the progress of your application, payment details and copies of correspondence...

...and much, much more.

All your student finance needs at your fingertips.

studentfinance **direct**

www.studentfinancedirect.co.uk

Part Three

How much will it cost?

How much

Financial support available for Scottish students studying in the UK

If you are a Scottish student taking a full-time course at HNC level or above, the support you can claim depends on:
- i) where you are studying;
- ii) the course you want to do; and
- iii) your personal circumstances.

To find out the amount available and how to obtain it go to the Student Awards Agency for Scotland (SAAS) website (**www.saas.gov.uk**) or phone them on **0845 111 1711**.

Tuition Fees – You may get free tuition if you are Scottish, studying in Scotland and you apply to SAAS to pay your full tuition fees direct to your college or university. If you are studying elsewhere in the UK, the amount they pay will depend on your or your family's income (or both). New arrangements being introduced in England mean that higher education institutions in England can charge tuition fees of up to £3,000 for new students starting university in 2006-2007. Eligible Scottish students and EU students, studying at an institution in Scotland will continue to get free tuition.

Student loans – For most students, the main support for living costs will be through the student loan, which will be partly income-assessed. You can choose how much of a loan you want – up to a maximum amount. The amount you can apply for depends on your personal circumstances but you could get roughly £4,000 a year. You should apply to SAAS if you want the loan and they will send your information to the Student Loans Company (SLC). You will not have to start repaying your loan until after you leave your course, have found a job and are earning over £15,000 a year.

Bursaries – Young Scottish students from low income families can get a Young Students' Bursary of up to £2,395 instead of part of the loan – so it reduces the amount of loan you need to take out. Scottish students studying elsewhere in the UK can get a Young Students' Outside Scotland Bursary of up to £545 on top of any loan they are entitled to.

Grants – Depending on your personal circumstances you may be able to apply to SAAS for extra help. For example, if you have travelling expenses, if you are a lone parent or you face extra costs to do your course because of a disability. You can get detailed information about these grants from the SAAS website (**www.saas.gov.uk**).

Graduate Endowment
You may have to pay the Graduate Endowment **after** you graduate. The amount you will pay is set when you start your course – at the moment it's just over £2,000 – but a lot of people are exempt from paying it. To find out if you're one of them, go to the SAAS website.

Other sources of financial help
There may be other sources of funding to help Scottish students while they are studying (for example Hardship or Childcare Funds). You can get more information about these from the SAAS website.

23

How much will it cost?

Let's not beat about the bush. You're thinking about going to university or college, or you might have already applied, but it's never really clear how much it's going to cost. So, what are the expenses? How much is it going to cost? How much cash will your parents have to lay out? Will it mean running up huge debts?

However, with student finance, simple questions rarely get a simple answer. There is no flat-rate pricing system – it's a complex mixture of variable charges and subsidies. But let's set out some basic guidelines. Yes, students do finish university and college with large debts – around £10,000 is not uncommon. And that figure will get higher when tuition fees increase.

So where does all the money go?

There are three major types of expense facing students. These are:

- tuition fees;
- living costs;
- debt repayments.

Fees

First, tuition fees – also known as top-up fees or variable fees. Tuition fees for 2005 will be £1,175 per year, although anyone with a family income below £32,744 will get some subsidy. A student from a household with an income below £22,010 won't have to pay anything. From 2006, fees will rise to £3,000 per year, but will be paid back in instalments after a student has graduated and is working. This means that a student from a middle-income family will be paying back fees of £9,000 after three years.

Living costs

Living costs will be your biggest expense at university or college, because you have to buy food and have a roof over your head like anyone else. And spending of around £7,000 per year is not unlikely. Accommodation is likely to cost between £50 and £100 per week, depending on factors such as local property prices. There will also be a combined shopping list of other expenses, such as food, utility bills and travel. As a basic cost, with no luxuries, this will be about £100 per week.

The government has estimated that average basic living costs and accommodation amount to £3,665 per year, plus an additional £3,232 for entertainment and non-study-related travel.

Debts

Interest-free loans are available from the Student Loans Company to help cover these living costs – with the total amount of such loans owed by students standing at over £14 billion. Loans are repaid directly from monthly pay, like income tax, once a student has graduated and begun work. The repayments start in April, in the year following graduation, and only when the former student is earning the equivalent of £15,000 or more per year. The deduction is based on 9 per cent of income above the £15,000 threshold.

In terms of a 'cost', the only money to be repaid is the amount borrowed – repayments only rise in line with inflation and there is no interest charge. Students can repay loans early by making extra payments. More than a quarter of the £622 million paid last year were early payments.

But there is a gap between these interest-free loans and how much students need to survive. Although many students will be working part time to bridge this gap they are also likely to borrow money, either in the form of bank loans, overdrafts or credit cards. Paying off a bank loan of £3,000, over three years, will mean repayments of about £92 per month. That will be on top of the repayments for the student loan – and, of course, many students will have borrowed higher amounts.

The shift to deferred payments for tuition fees will lessen the burden while students are at university or college, but will add to the financial squeeze afterwards, when they're working.

How much students will need to borrow will also be influenced by how much financial support they can gain. Although there are all kinds of sums promised for grants and bursaries, they are mostly targeted at low-income families, and many middle-income families will miss out. If a two-parent family has a combined income of £43,000, the student will not get any support and his or her parents will be liable for paying £2,225 per year, including fees and a contribution towards living costs.

These are real costs, which will have to be paid for three years. And there are other less tangible costs, such as lost earnings. How much salary could a young person have taken home in three years?

But, before getting into the detail of costs, it's worth flipping the question the other way. Paying rent and living expenses will represent one of the biggest costs for a student. But, whether you are a student or not, you'd still need to live somewhere and pay bills. So these costs are not exclusive to going to university or college.

And, an even more important question to ask is how much it might cost not to go to university or college. The high-status jobs are overwhelmingly going to go to graduates. There are exceptions, but the great weight of evidence shows that graduates have the richest pickings in the jobs market.

Students might have debts, but once they've graduated they'll have the potential to earn more than enough to clear them.

24

Living costs

Even though tuition fees have grabbed many of the headlines about student finance, in terms of pounds and pence, the biggest expense for a student is going to be the basic living costs – accommodation, food and travel. And this is where student loans, financial support from parents and borrowing from banks is going to be spent.

It is not going to be cheap. For your parents, sending you away for three years, regardless of whether you are a student or not, is going to inflict some serious pain in the wallet region. And the amount that it's going to cost will vary greatly between students, just as living costs vary between other groups of teenagers. If you only wear designer clothes and travel everywhere by taxi you are going to have a different level of running costs from someone who shops around for a bargain and uses a bus pass.

According to the government, there has been a 'substantial rise in students' standard of living', which is reflected in higher spending. It has shown that, while the basic living costs facing students are £3,665 per year, another £3,232 is being spent on entertainment and non-study-related travel.

This is going to be in excess of the loan available, even if you qualify for the full amount. Which means that either your parents will be forking out to cover the cost – or, more likely, you will have a part-time job during term-time and use credit cards and over-drafts.

In thinking about the size of spending on living costs, there are certain factors that will influence the likely expense.

Accommodation

Rent is going to be one of the biggest expenses. In fact, it's going to take a great big chunk out of your annual income. As with house prices, there will be a huge variation in the cost of renting. It depends on where the property is, how big it is and all the other factors that affect value. If you go to a university or college in a city with high property prices and you choose a massive flat, then your accommodation costs are going to be radically different from someone sharing with an improbably large number of other students in a flat in a cheap part of a low-cost town.

But when you begin considering the different factors in the cost of somewhere to live, the first decision is whether it's university or college accommodation or private rental. For new students, university or college accommodation, in which you share with other students, isn't just a roof over your head – it's an instant social life. So, when you look at the relative costs, it's worth factoring in such intangibles as not being Mr or Ms No-Mates watching a portable television in a bedsit on your own.

As an example of how costs vary, a big university in northern England says its average cost for staying in university halls of residence is £83 per week, while the university's self-catering flats are £63 per week. In comparison, privately rented accommodation in the same city was averaging £56 per week, based on four people sharing. While this is slightly cheaper than the university accommodation, there will be additional costs for utility bills. And if you're self-catering, or in a privately rented flat, then you'll also have to add on the cost of the weekly food run at the supermarket.

Renting also involves a hefty initial outlay, with payments in advance and a deposit against damages. And it's worth noting that getting deposits returned when a tenancy finishes has become an irritating difficulty for many students.

It's also important to consider what you're getting for your money. University and college accommodation has improved in quality in recent years and is no longer going to feel like a rather Spartan boarding school. Student rooms now often have their own bathrooms, plus facilities such as an internet connection. Having your own bathroom might not sound like luxury, but in a shared rented house, you'd be more likely to be sharing a bathroom between four. University and college accommodation might also have added extras, such as washing machines, television in a common room, a computer room and games rooms.

Apart from differences in accommodation costs between universities and colleges, there are also differences within institutions. For example, at a university in the south-west of England, the weekly cost of a hall of residence ranges between £88 per week and £115 per week (2004–05 prices), with differences such as whether rooms have en suite bathrooms. Self-catering accommodation, for a single room, ranges from an 'economy' price of £45 per week up to £100 per week for an en suite. Just to show how difficult it is to generalize about accommodation costs, there are even differences within an individual hall of residence, depending on the facilities in rooms.

At a university in the north-east, within one of its halls of residence, there are rooms costing £72 per week or £98 per week, with the cheaper rooms having a washbasin in the room, while the higher price is for an en suite study bedroom. Over the course of the year, the total is £2,262 against £3,648 – so if you can put up with only having a washbasin you can save more than £1,000 per year. Self-catering accommodation at the same university also has a range of prices, between £45 per week and £75 per week (for the 2004–05 academic year).

University and college accommodation offices will also be able to tell you the likely cost of local privately-rented flats but, as with house prices, these can change from month to month depending on the buoyancy or otherwise of the local property market. If you want to get regional comparisons on the cost of renting, there are plenty of estate agents' websites where you can check the current asking prices.

Geography

There are also different ways of looking at affordability when it comes to choosing a university or college.

For instance, the Royal Bank of Scotland produces an index of student living costs. In 2004 it found that the average student was spending £66 per week on rent, with London the most expensive place at £81 per week, and Liverpool the cheapest at £52 per week. And it showed the difference in living expenses for students. In Aberdeen, weekly spending on rent and basic living costs was £140 per week, while in Cambridge it was £227 per week.

But the survey also includes a 'best value' league table of universities, taking into account both the cost of living and accommodation and also the potential to work part time. On this ranking, Glasgow was best value, with students spending £181 per week, but able to offset this with weekly earnings of £103.

This league table might mean breaking some bad news. Students don't only have to work on their studies, they also are likely to have a part-time job as well. And the Royal Bank of Scotland student living index shows that even in places where students spend less – such as in Durham (weekly expenditure £172) – they can still be less well-off, because average earnings are only £57 per week. This mixture of costs and earning power claims that the difference between students at Glasgow and Durham could be over £1,100.

This student cost of living index also shows how 'expensive' locations can be offset by greater opportunities for part-time work. So, on this calculation, London is more cost effective than Nottingham, and Oxford is more cost effective than York.

Even though such rankings might be contested, it shows there are different ways of looking at the bigger picture of expense. As with everything to do with student finance, it's a question of looking at how the immediate costs can be balanced by the short-term subsidies and long-term benefits.

Food and living costs

If accommodation is the biggest single weekly expense, there's also going to be an assortment of other living costs that will have to be covered, such as food, clothes, travel and entertainment. This is going to vary depending on how much luxury you need in your life – but this list of combined 'other' expenses is likely to add up to a total about the same as your weekly rent.

The National Union of Students says that students will need to budget for about £25 to £30 per week on food, £25 per week on socializing, £14 per week on travel and £10 per week towards clothes. An estimate from a central London university says students will spend about £35 on food and housekeeping, £25 for entertainment, £12 for travel and £5 to £10 for clothes each week.

A national survey of student attitudes found that students were spending more than £20 per week on a combination of mobile phones, clothes, DVDs and music. About £35 was spent each week on going out and drinking and £31 was spent on food.

On these prices it's not going to be a life of wild spending and retail therapy. But it gives an indication of the basic level of spending that will be necessary. And these averages can be changed drastically by individual circumstances, such as if you have a long, expensive journey into university or college or if you have a designer clothes habit that you can't shake off. But, as a starting point, this means spending about £80–£100 per week, in addition to rent.

Gas, electricity, water and phone bills

If you're in university or college accommodation you probably won't have to pay separate gas, electricity and water bills. But if you're renting privately, this is another unavoidable cost. The National Union of Students suggests a typical weekly expenditure of about £10.

Another wild card in estimating costs is the mobile phone. If you're someone who lives on the phone, then it's going to take up more of your available spending power. If you're restrained enough only to use it in emergencies, then it's going to be much cheaper. But as a working estimate, let's call it £6 per week.

With all these utility bills, there are usually cheaper alternatives if you shop around. Energy suppliers can be changed with a phone call if you can find a cheaper deal. There are also discounts from phone companies, which will give savings from the standard call charges.

Course expenses

Along with all the stuff about paying gas bills, it's important not to forget the point of the exercise, which is to go to university or college to get a degree. And this has its own costs, separate to the fees. You'll need books and course materials, which won't always be available from the library.

The students' union in a northern university estimates course costs at about £5 per week, and the National Union of Students says it's about £8 per week. Across a term, the Unite/Mori survey of student life says that students are spending £70 on course books, and another £56 on items such as photocopying, stationery and course-related trips, which would push up the weekly spending on course materials to over £12 per week.

Tuition fees

Under the current system of charges, students starting university or college in autumn 2005 will have to pay £1,175 per year in tuition fees. There is financial support available to help pay fees, with the amount of support dependent on family income.

If the combined household income is below £22,010, there is financial support to pay the entire fee. If the combined household income is between £22,010 and £32,744, students will get some support, on a sliding scale up to the full amount. The more that parents earn, the less support their student children will receive. The actual average fee paid last year was £575. If the combined household income is above £32,744, there is no financial support available and the student and his or her family will be liable for the full amount.

There are some details to add to this. The household income is not just the gross amount earned by parents and the student themselves. Other financial commitments can be taken into account. For any other dependent child £1,025 is deducted from the household income total (which includes the earnings of unmarried live-in partners). And students do not have to include any part-time or holiday earnings from jobs. If a parent receives maintenance payments from a former partner, this also is not included in the total income to be assessed. This income, taking into account any deductions, is described as the 'residual' income.

Apart from a few gap year students, the intake of new students in 2005 will be the last who will pay these up-front tuition fees. But these students entering in 2005 will continue with this payment system until they graduate in 2008.

Fees changing in 2006

All of these arrangements are about to change – and students intending to enter English universities and colleges in 2006 will have a very different system.

The fees will be much higher – increasing almost threefold to a maximum of £3,000 per year. But they will no longer have to be paid up front when the student is still at university or college. Instead, tuition fees will be repaid from the year after students have left university or college and are earning at least £15,000 per year.

In terms of cost, this will mean that students could leave university or college owing £9,000 in tuition fees, instead of about £3,600, which is paid in advance under the current charges. Even though the total cost of fees will be greater, those arguing for the deferred payment system say it will be more affordable for young people – and will make university and college courses free at the point of delivery.

There is a commitment that this maximum fee level will only increase with inflation until 2010. And if fees have not been paid back in full after 25 years they will be written off.

These new arrangements will be accompanied by a new form of subsidy. A grant of up to £2,700 per year will be available, paid in instalments at the beginning of each term, which will not have to be paid back. And it's expected that about half of all full-time students will be able to claim at least some amount of grant.

To make matters more complicated, tuition fees will no longer be a fixed amount for all universities and colleges or all courses. They can't charge above £3,000, but there might be a lower charge for some courses at some universities and colleges. In theory, fees could be anything from zero up to the £3,000 upper limit. The signs so far have been that most courses are going to be charged at the full amount – but it's difficult to forecast in advance what kind of pricing structure might emerge.

This is a new and untried system, and the whole question of how cost might influence demand from students remains uncertain. And it won't really be known until variable fees have been around for a few years.

Universities and colleges themselves face tough decisions over this. If they opt for reduced fees, will it put off students who don't want to be seen to be attending a lower-status institution? Or will universities and colleges who charge the maximum find themselves being ignored as students go bargain hunting for cheaper courses?

In terms of what it will cost students in repayments after gradua-tion, the government has produced a guide to costs as a proportion of income. The tuition fee repayment will be wrapped up with payment for the student loan, and a single deduction will be made by the Inland Revenue each month from the former student's salary, along with other payments such as National Insurance and income tax.

- at £15,000, no repayment, 0% of income;
- at £18,000, monthly payment £22, 1.5% of income;
- at £20,000, monthly payment £37, 2.3% of income;
- at £22,000, monthly payment £52, 2.9% of income;
- at £24,000, monthly payment £67, 3.4% of income;
- at £25,000, monthly payment £75, 3.6% of income.

Fees for gap year students

Taking a gap year between school and university or college has become an established pattern for many young people. And there were complaints that, if students this year decided to take a gap year, they would return to face the higher tuition fees that will be intro-duced for 2006.

So, an exception has been made for this particular group of gap year students. Even though they will be beginning university or college in autumn 2006, they will be treated under the conditions of the autumn 2005 fees system. This means that they will be charged at the present £1,175 per year for tuition fees, rather than the new rate of £3,000. It also means that the benefits they can claim will be based on the system that is being replaced. As such they will not qualify for the non-repayable grant of up to £2,700 per year.

Fees for trainee teachers

Students on postgraduate teacher training courses (PGCEs), which usually follow a three-year degree course, are currently exempt from paying any tuition fees. This is because the government wants to encourage more people into teaching – and they do not want potential teachers to be put off by having to pay another year's tuition fee.

26

Loan repayments

When you're trying to work out how much it's going to cost to go to university or college, you have to be ready to take a long-term perspective – because the costs of going to university or college, such as fees and living costs, are not going to be paid out of your own pocket while you're still a student. You're going to borrow money to cover these costs – and after you've graduated you'll have to pay it back. And you'll be paying it back for many years to come.

There has been much concern about this student borrowing, with fears that students are graduating with a mountain of debt. New lending increased sharply last year to £2.7 billion, making the total amount of money now owed to the Student Loans Company £14.6 billion.

But it's worth taking a step back from the headlines and thinking, in the context of 'what it costs', as to how you'll be paying back the money borrowed while at university or college.

Loans to students to cover living costs are provided by the Student Loans Company. So, when you read about the cost of accommodation and bills, student loans will be an important source of support. These official loans from the Student Loans Company are not to be confused with borrowing from banks or credit card companies. And the big difference is in the level of charges for repayment.

While a bank will charge a commercial rate of interest (perhaps with some kind of student discount), the Student Loans Company lends money at a rate that is meant to be effectively interest free – with the repayment only rising to cover the inflation rate. This is worth repeating, because it's a complicated arrangement. When you borrow a student loan from the Student Loans Company, in effect, there is no real cost to that borrowing. You have to repay the money you've borrowed, but you're not paying any additional interest charge. Instead, you pay back the money in instalments once you've graduated and started working – so a 'student loan' isn't actually repaid when you're a student.

The repayment process begins in the April after you've graduated. So, if you graduate in the summer, you don't pay anything back through the autumn and winter. Then, from April, the repayments are taken as monthly deductions from your salary – once you've reached the equivalent of earning £15,000 per year.

There is a sliding scale for repayments – the more you earn, the more you pay back – based on deducting 9 per cent of income above the £15,000 per year threshold. It's taken directly from your monthly salary along with tax and National Insurance. There are no options on when the money is repaid – you can't say that you want to defer the monthly deductions. When you reach the income threshold, the payment system kicks in. If you don't reach the repayment threshold of £15,000, you don't start paying off the loan.

But if you leave the country, or start working overseas, you're still obliged to make the repayments. And you'll be expected to contact the Student Loans Company to make arrangements for payment.

If you're self-employed, and so not getting a monthly salary from an employer, the repayments are deducted through the self-assessment tax return.

If you leave a course before it's finished – and so don't graduate – you will have to repay what you've borrowed.

And if you're a runaway financial success, and desperate to clear your debts, you can pay off your loan early by sending extra payments to the Student Loans Company. This is more popular than you might expect. Figures last year showed that more than a quarter of the £622 million in student loan repayments were paid earlier than needed.

There can also be differences in loan repayments for teacher training graduates, as part of the government's efforts to encourage people to train as teachers in shortage subjects. There has been a pilot scheme, running until summer 2005, which has seen the government picking up the tab for loan repayments for teachers in subjects including science and maths. And if you're considering teacher training, check with the university or college to see whether there are any further discounts in loan repayment.

To look on the gloomy side, if you die before the loan is repaid, it is cancelled. And it's also cancelled if someone becomes permanently disabled and unfit for work.

27

Debt repayments

When people talk about student finance, the phrase 'student debt' is not usually far behind. Paying back loans to the Student Loans Company is only one part of the debt equation – and there is a much more expensive side to this. Students are unlikely to survive without borrowing more than the amount available from the Student Loans Company – and there is no shortage of offers from other lenders to fill the gap.

Borrowing from the bank or running up debts on credit cards will have real costs in terms of interest and charges (unlike the interest-free lending for student loans from the Student Loans Company). If you're trying to work out a financial price tag for a university or college degree, the cost of paying off debt is going to be more significant than the headline-grabbing cost of the tuition fees.

A large number of means-tested students won't even pay tuition fees, but most students will be paying off debts for years after they leave university or college. And how much you'll have to pay will depend on how much you borrow.

Banks will offer deals such as interest-free overdrafts to students and discounted loans. And there will be reduced-rate deals for newly-graduated students, as a kind of introductory offer to the real world. But, like all teaser deals on any kind of lending, these special offers run out, and money owed will have to be given back. And, as an example, if you have to pay back a bank loan of £3,000, repayments over three years will be about £92 per month. You can stretch out payments over a longer period, but that means paying more interest.

If you had to pay the bank £5,000 over three years, it would be around £154 per month. And if you'd run up a debt of £10,000, you'd have to pay more than £300 per month. If this repayment were stretched out over five years, you'd only pay £196 per month. But you would be paying more than £1,700 in interest alone. This example is calculated at a competitive personal loan rate – if that 10 grand were on a credit card, the cost would be even higher.

So how much are students borrowing while they are at university or college?

According to an annual survey from Barclays, average student debt increased by 500 per cent in the decade between 1994 and 2004. Back in 1994, the average student left university or college owing £2,212. By 2004, the annual Barclays survey showed that students were leaving with debts of £12,069.

The largest part of this debt would involve interest-free borrowing from the Student Loans Company, along with overdrafts, credit cards, bank loans and money borrowed from parents. The bank attributed this increase in debt to a rising cost of living, the introduction of tuition fees, and the removal of grants. And it forecasts, rather gloomily, that for students starting in 2007 a three-year degree course could leave them with average debts of £33,000. The government has rejected this figure, but it suggests how the scale of debt is likely to increase in the next few years, as higher tuition fees are implemented.

Without looking into the crystal ball, the current figure of graduates leaving university or college with debts of over £12,000 shows that many students are borrowing beyond what's available from the Student Loans Company. The Unite/Mori survey found that students had a wide spread of borrowing. The average student with an overdraft owed £1,100; those with credit card debts owed £1,170; those who used hire purchase deals owed £1,860; and those with bank loans owed £4,500.

A survey from the NatWest bank found that students were leaving with average debts of £12,180 – and that many students expected to be repaying these debts for more than a decade. Taken in isolation, paying off this debt might be affordable, once the ex-student is earning a decent living in a full-time job. But there have also been concerns that if student debts are still being paid off a decade after graduation, then it's going to be yet another financial drag on young people trying to buy a house or wanting to settle down and start their own families.

This argument says that becoming a student means entering a culture of borrowing, with the student loan representing a kind of mini-mortgage which will be swiftly followed by a real mortgage. But there are arguments against this. The government says that forecasts of spiralling debts overlook the planned increases in grants and subsidies.

Also, you don't have to go to university or college to build up a credit card debt – and young people generally have an increasing tendency to use credit, regardless of their academic intentions. While we talk about the rise in student debt, it's part of a bigger picture in which throughout society there has been a sharp rise in consumer debt.

Many students will have part-time jobs to minimize their borrowing. And, just as you hear nightmare stories about individual students who have borrowed ridiculously large amounts, there are also students who will have been canny enough to leave with a minimum of debts. Because, even if the large majority of a student's debt is owed to the interest-free Student Loans Company, a few thousand on the credit card can be hard work to pay off.

Unlike the student loans, credit card repayments won't be troubled by whether you're working or not – the bill is going to be there every month. And, even if you use some fancy footwork with zero per cent interest deals, at some point the money will need to be paid off.

When we're in a sombre mood about student cash, it's also worth raising the question of students who drop out of university or college. Financial pressures have been cited as one of the main reasons that students leave higher education before finishing. But in cash terms, this early departure is the worst of both worlds, leaving young people with the debts to repay, but without the extra earning power that comes with a degree.

It's also not as unusual as might be imagined. About one in seven students who begin university or college courses drop out – and in some universities and colleges this figure rises to over one in three.

There are over a dozen universities and colleges where more than a quarter of students will be expected to drop out. There are also some universities and colleges, particularly the most prestigious, where almost no one drops out.

But as a cautionary tale, it's worth thinking about this risk in advance. Because these figures suggest that a considerable number of young people have paid out for tuition fees and borrowed a student loan, but then changed their minds. And even though they've changed their minds, they're still going to have to make the repayments, without the compensation of having got the degree.

What will parents have to pay?

Parents are going to look anxiously at how much they will be expected to pay towards sending an offspring to university or college. Depending on family income, this can be anything between zero and £2,470 per year. Parents with children already at university or college, however, might say that this is only what they are required to pay – and that in fact they give much greater levels of financial support.

Parents are expected to make a means-tested level of contributions to students, with higher earners paying higher contributions. At present, the cut-off point is £22,010. If parents' combined, pre-tax incomes are less than this, they won't have to make any contribution. If they earn more than this they will make contributions based on a sliding scale. These will first be expected to cover tuition fees, up to £1,175. Any contributions over this figure will reduce the level of interest-free loan available from the Student Loans Company.

This applies to parents who earn more than £32,745. Up to this income, parents will only have to pay towards fees; above this amount, they will then pay towards their child's living costs in the form of replacing part of the available student loan with a parental contribution.

The annual parental contribution towards their children's living costs can be up to:

- £1,295 for students living away from home at a London university or college;
- £1,050 for students living away from home outside London;
- £830 for students living at home with their parents.

In the final year, where funding is provided for fewer weeks, the amounts that parents will have to pay are lowered:

- £1,120 for students living away from home at a London university or college;
- £910 for students living away from home outside London;
- £725 for students living at home with their parents.

This means that the maximum parental contributions will be to cover the tuition fee, £1,175, plus up to £1,295 towards living costs.

For a parent to be liable to pay this full amount of both fee and contribution towards living costs, the household income would have to be above:

- £45,048 for a student living away from home at a London university or college;
- £42,720 for a student living away from home at a university or college outside London;
- £40,630 for a student living at home.

This means that the maximum contribution for a parent would be:

- £2,470 for a student living away from home at a London university or college;
- £2,225 for a student living away from home at a university or college outside London;
- £2,005 for a student living at home.

This is a means-tested sliding scale, and uses the 'see-saw' model that is common to much of student finances. As parental income goes down, so the level of support rises. And the other way around, as parental income climbs upwards, so the financial assistance is lowered.

So a student at a London university or college from a family earning up to £32,745 would get the full student loan, worth £5,175. While a student from a better-off family, earning more than £42,720, would only get £3,880 in the student loan – and the parent would be expected to pay the remaining £1,295.

Between these points the loan available and the expected parental contribution are adjusted on a sliding scale, according to family income. And the calculation is based on families having to make a parental contribution worth £1 for every £9.50 of income above the threshold of £22,010.

If you want to work out your own circumstances, under the current funding arrangements, it's a case of subtracting £22,010 from your income, and then dividing that by 9.5 and adding £45 (the £45 being the amount liable to be paid if income is exactly on the threshold).

Confused? I don't blame you. And there are even more complications. The changeover in tuition fees will have an impact on parental contributions.

At present, once you've run your calculator over your income, your expected level of contribution will be taken into consideration for the means-testing of tuition fees as well as eligibility for loans. Under the current arrangements, the parental contribution is first used towards paying all or some of the £1,175 tuition fee.

But from 2006, there will be no more up-front fees, and repayments will be made through deductions from salary after students have graduated. The government has presented this as a benefit to middle-income families, who will no longer be putting their parental contributions into covering up-front tuition fees. But parents will still be expected to pay a means-tested proportion of student loans.

Reality check

These figures are the official amounts that parents are expected to contribute. But no one is going to come around to make sure that parents sign the cheques. If you have parents who are loaded, but want to spend all their cash on flash cars, mortgages and skiing holidays, the government isn't going to step in to make them give you your fair share.

This problem of depending on unreliable parents has been raised by student unions, who complain that students can be left in the lurch. Having rich parents will reduce the amount of loan available to students, but if the parents don't hand over their expected contributions, then these 'rich' students will lose out.

But anyone who has ever been to university or college will know that parental contributions can also be much greater than the required level. Insurers say that about one in five students now have their own cars, with a large number of these motors being given as presents by parents. Parents will also look at their required level of support, perhaps a couple of thousand a year, and say that this is an unrealistically low estimate of what they'll really contribute.

They might have had to stump up for the deposit on a rented flat, paid train fares, sent extra cash to tide students over when they were waiting for a loan to arrive. Parents might want to limit their children's level of debt, and so prefer to lend from the Bank of Parent instead. Surveys have suggested that many students have borrowed in excess of £1,000 from their parents.

There are expensive items such as laptops that are now pretty standard for students – and again, these are likely to be funded by parents. And other equipment taken from the family home to university or college, such as a spare television set or radio, will represent another type of subsidy. And all these expenses are going to be in addition to the official parental contribution towards tuition fees and loans.

To be realistic, how long would you expect to survive in London on less than £5,000 per year? It might just about cover the rent and bills, but the extras are going to depend on someone else helping out – and if it isn't the credit card, it's likely to be Mum and Dad.

29

Part-time students

Fees

If you're one of the growing number of students studying part time you'll have a different set of costs from full-time students. There are tuition fees for part-time students, but at present these are likely to be below the £1,175 rate for full-time students. Unlike the fixed fee for full-time students, universities and colleges have been able to decide their own fees for part-time students.

This makes it harder to generalize about the likely cost. But surveys show that a high proportion of part-time students are paying somewhere between £400 and £1,000 per year. The average fee, in terms of a full-time equivalent place, is £998, says research for the Department for Education and Skills.

Course costs, such as books and travel, are estimated at £246 per year. But the DfES survey reported that this was distorted by some very high figures for a few students – and that a more typical figure for course costs was about £110 per year. The total cost of course-related expenses was estimated to average £486 per year.

The impact of such costs on part-time students will vary greatly, because there are very different groups using part-time university and college courses. A majority of part-time students are in work and almost two-thirds are in full-time jobs. For these students, the fees and incidental costs will be affordable, especially when about half of them get all their fees paid by their employer. A quarter of part-time students have an income above £40,000 per year.

Most part-time students tend to be older and are likely to have their own accommodation. And if their employer picks up the bill for the fees, then this becomes a very cost-effective way of getting a degree, with few of the debts and expenses facing full-time students.

But there is another group among part-time students who will face a tougher time. About one in three qualify for full financial support and four in ten have an income of less than £15,000 per year.

Changes in 2006

An unresolved question about the costs facing part-time students will be what will happen when full-time tuition fees are overhauled in 2006.

Full-time tuition fees will not have to be paid until after students have graduated. But, for part-time students, there has been no suggestion so far that they will be able to defer repayment until after graduation. If it takes six years for a part-time student to complete a degree, will the government allow them those extra years before expecting a repayment on the fees?

Or will part-timers become the only students who still have to pay their fees in advance, when everyone else has been relieved of this burden? This becomes even more problematic if the fees for part-time students are pushed up in line with full-time rates. Would part-time students be ready to pay £3,000 per year up front?

Higher education institutions, some of which now have a majority of part-time students, are concerned that if they hike the part-time fees it will deter people from applying. But if they don't increase the part-time fees then, in effect, they're going to be forced to subsidize students, which would mean there was a financial penalty for attracting part-time students.

When the government is so committed to widening access to higher education, it would be difficult for it to be seen to be closing the door on just the type of second-chance, mature students they want to bring in. For typical part-time students, in their thirties and with a job, possibly also supporting a family, there might not be any other practical way to go to university or college.

Financial assistance

In terms of balancing costs and support, it is unlikely that the financial support available will cover the expenses, as many students won't get much from the means-tested assistance. To help with tuition fees, there is £590 for students on a course equivalent to 50–59 per cent of a full-time course, £710 on a course equivalent to 60–74 per cent of a full-time course and £885 for students on courses at least 75 per cent of a full-time course.

These maximum amounts are available for students with incomes below £14,970, with reduced amounts available up to an income threshold of £22,000, at which point the support ceases. But, even if they don't get anything in support, part-time students who are working and might already have their own homes are going to be spared the epic scale of borrowing which faces the full-time student.

If they have to pay £1,000 per year, but are able to keep working, it's not going to have such a drastic impact on their finances. And if, as is often the case, their employer is covering the fees, then this becomes a highly affordable investment.

30

'Independent' and mature students

Not all students are going to fit into the model of being young people who have just left school and are leaving home and parents for the first time. So, if you left home many years ago, how much will it cost to send yourself to university or college? And how would you qualify for financial support?

When it comes to assessing how much such students have to pay, there is a separate category called 'independent' students. This independent status will require proof. As the rules from the Department for Education and Skills say: 'You will not be able to claim independent status just because you do not get on with your parents or because you do not live with them.' This restriction is because, if everyone could declare themselves independent, then parents would be let off the hook from making contributions.

Independent students have their own earnings, rather than their parents', assessed. And since most students will not have much in the way of an income, they will stand to gain from any benefits available. Only about 35 per cent of students who depend on their parents have all their tuition fees covered, while this figure rises sharply to 87 per cent of independent students.

While only 9 per cent of independent students pay the full fee, 48 per cent of dependent students whose parents have been means-tested have to pay the full fee. So it's not surprising that the independent status for students is only carefully awarded.

The category of independent students includes those who are aged 25 or over, those who are married, and those who have supported themselves for at least three years. Students will have to show evidence that they have supported themselves for this length of time, such as P60s showing employment, or documents showing that they were claiming benefit. These students will not have their parental incomes taken into account.

Self-evidently, if a student's parents have died, this will also put the student into the independent category. This is also the case if there is 'permanent estrangement' from parents, or if there is no practical way in which the parents could be contacted. If a student wants to claim independent status because of such a permanent family separation it will require some kind of supporting evidence, such as a letter from a doctor, school or social worker, describing the nature of this estrangement. The guidelines also suggest that this separation should mean that there has been no contact with parents in the previous year.

And if you have been living in care, whether through a local authority or voluntary organization, you will also have independent status.

Tuition fees

When working out how much an independent student will have to contribute to his or her fees, or how much interest-free loan will be available, there are differences between single and married students.

Independent students who are single will have any income above £10,250 per year taken into account, excluding any part-time work while they are at university or college. If they earn less than this, they won't have to pay their own tuition fees and will receive the maximum student loan available. And any income above this level will, on a sliding scale, mean paying more of the tuition fee, or all of it, and reducing the amount of student loan available.

As with parental contributions, this sliding scale is based on £1 in contribution for every £9.50 earned above this threshold, plus £45. This means that an independent student earning £20,985 will be liable to pay the full £1,175 tuition fees. Any income above this level will reduce the level of student grant available.

Students who are married or living with a partner will have their partner's income assessed, in the same way as other students have their parents' incomes assessed. These payments, as with parental contributions, begin once the partner's income reaches £22,010. And, once again, the formula for working out contributions is based on £1 for every £9.50 in income above £22,010, plus £45.

So if an independent student is married to someone earning £35,000 per year, the working partner will have to contribute £1,412 per year. If the working partner is earning £40,000, he or she will have to contribute £1,939. Both these amounts are above the current £1,175 maximum for tuition fees. So once this amount has been allocated to cover tuition fees, the remainder will be taken from the amount available in interest-free loans.

This would mean, if you were a student with a partner earning £40,000, your partner would be expected to contribute £764 towards your living costs – and this amount would be deducted from the loan available.

Student loans

As with students who have support from their parents, the loan is in two elements – 75 per cent which isn't means-tested and is available to everyone, and 25 per cent which is means-tested. This means-tested element of the loan is available on a sliding scale. The more an independent student's partner earns, the less of the interest-free loan will be available.

31

Scotland

The tuition fees system and the funding of students has been in a state of constant change in recent years – and one aspect of this has been the way that different parts of the United Kingdom have been developing their own student finance arrangements. But it's further complicated because Scottish universities and colleges will not only be attended by students from Scotland, there will also be students from other parts of the UK, which means that the systems have to overlap. For a definition of what it means to be a Scottish student, see Chapter 19, page 96.

This has created some problems – and it's a fair bet that disputes will continue to rumble on. Because it can mean that students at the same university or college are paying different levels of fees for the same course, depending on where they're from in the UK.

The system being introduced in England is about creating a market, with different universities and colleges being able to charge different fees. And this will take it further away from a Scottish system that shows no enthusiasm for such an approach.

Tuition fees

The biggest difference so far has concerned tuition fees. While the English system has required tuition fees to be paid up front at the beginning of the academic year, the Scottish arrangement has been for a charge to be paid back after students graduate.

Sounds familiar? Yes, that's the system that England is moving towards in 2006. But, in the meantime, for students going to university or college in 2005 this means a different set of costs to consider.

If you are a student from Scotland, going to a Scottish university or college, then the tuition fee will be covered by the Scottish funding body, the Student Awards Agency for Scotland (SAAS). The tuition fee still exists, but while students are at university or college it's effectively invisible to the naked eye. The cost of the tuition fee is fully subsidized.

Instead, and as the outcome of a political compromise over fees, there is a 'graduate endowment' to be paid once students have graduated. This is a one-off payment in recognition of the benefits of higher education – and goes towards the support of future students. The repayments for the graduate endowment rise with inflation. For students who began their courses in Scottish universities and colleges in 2004–05, the endowment will be £2,154.

This can either be paid in a single lump sum or else all or part of the amount can be covered by an extended loan from the Student Loans Company, with repayments beginning in the April of the year following graduation.

There is a number of groups of students in Scotland who are exempt from paying the 'graduate endowment'. These include students who were independent of their parents at the start of the course, lone parents, disabled students, students who fail their courses, part-time students and those who have previously studied on a higher education degree course.

In terms of working out how much money you'll have to pay out initially, if you are a Scottish student at a Scottish university or college you can push tuition fees to one side for now. And your parents will have one less immediate expense to consider.

Student loans

But the other aspect of cost for students and their families will be living expenses – and the arrangements for loans to cover them. The loan has two elements: the first is a non-means-tested minimum that is available to all students, regardless of their family's income; the second part is a means-tested loan, made available depending on the student's family income.

This is where your parent (or your partner) will be expected to make a financial contribution. As the Student Awards Agency for Scotland says: 'We treat the contribution as part of each student's support and we will reduce the amount we pay by the amount of the contribution.'

It is a similar funding see-saw to the one in England where, as the parental contribution rises, the government support decreases. But, unlike in England, the first slice of the parental income will not go to cover tuition fees. Instead it will be applied to income-assessed grants, loans and then travelling expenses.

There are additional bursaries available to students in Scotland but, again, access to these decreases as income rises. The current point at which parents will be expected to contribute is an annual household income of £21,475.

The level of contribution rises with income above this level:

■ £436 per year for those earning £25,000;
■ £992 for those earning £30,000;
■ £2,103 for those earning £40,000;
■ £3,423 for those earning £50,000.

This earnings figure can be lowered if families qualify for deductions because of other expenses, such as other children in the household, or if a parent has a disability. But the big picture is that it is in parental contributions that most families will feel the expense. Parents earning a fairly modest income, perhaps £20,000 each, could be facing contributions in excess of £2,000.

Independent, married and mature students

There are separate arrangements for students who are no longer considered to be dependent on their parents and so whose contributions are no longer calculated on their parents' income. Students in

Scotland are defined as independent if they are aged 25 or over, the student's parents are dead, the student is married or has supported him or herself for three years.

This independent status is also given to students whose parents are out of contact, if the student has been in care up until going to university or college or if the student has been caring for a 'dependent child' for at least three years. For a single independent student, his or her own income will be assessed, in the way that other students might have their parents' income means-tested.

And for these single independent students, income from part-time jobs while they're at university or college isn't taken into account. Scholarships and sponsorships of up to £4,350 will also be disregarded, as will the first £4,350 if an employer carries on paying a student while he or she is studying. A student whose parents have died can receive up to £2,095 from a trust without having it taken into account in the means-testing.

Independent students who are married will have their partner's income assessed, rather than their parents' income. On this assessment scale, partners of married students have to make a financial contribution if their income is above £18,260. At £25,000, the contribution is £793; if they earn £30,000, they'll have to pay £1,349; at £40,000, the contribution is £2,460; and at £50,000, it's £3,781.

Scottish students at UK universities and colleges outside Scotland

The big financial question here for students will be how the differences in tuition fees will be funded. Will it cost more to go to English universities and colleges who demand tuition fees up front? And will Scottish students face the same hike in fees when tuition fees in England treble in 2006?

Scottish students who go to an English or a Welsh university or college will be liable to pay tuition fees at the same rate as other students. For students who are starting courses in 2005, this will mean paying fees in advance, at the current rate of £1,150. And whether this will be subsidized by the Student Awards Agency for Scotland will depend on the same means-tested assessment as the loans system – with parental contributions being required if household income is above £21,475.

The difference is that for Scottish students at Scottish universities or colleges this assessment will determine the availability of loans – but for Scottish students who are south of the border, this will also determine payment of tuition fees. And if after the means-testing, parents of Scottish students in England are required to make a contribution, then these payments will first be used to cover tuition fees. If the level of parental contribution is greater than the tuition fee, then this extra amount is then deducted from the loan available from the Student Loans Company.

For a Scottish student at an English university or college outside London, the maximum loan is £4,095, of which £1,960 is non-income-assessed and goes to everyone. The remaining amount, £2,135, is based on the means-tested assessment – with the most available to the students from homes with the lowest incomes.

So your parents will face costs on a sliding scale between zero and £2,135 (slightly more if the university or college is in London) for the student loan, plus between zero and £1,150 for tuition fees – with means-testing determining how much each family will have to contribute.

Changes to tuition fees for 2006

The overhaul of the tuition fees system in England will also mean a financial shake-up for cross-border students. And the dust hasn't entirely settled on how the arrangements will work.

From September 2006, tuition fees in England are going to increase to a maximum of £3,000 per year. This won't affect students who have already begun courses, but it will apply to Scottish students who start courses in England next year.

These new fees won't be paid up front any more, but they will still be higher than their Scottish equivalents. The Scottish executive has indicated that it will cover the extra costs 'to ensure that Scottish students are not disadvantaged as a result of the Westminster proposals'.

English students at Scottish universities and colleges

The changes in 2006 could be less good news for English students at Scottish universities and colleges, because there have been indications that these students will face higher fees, even though Scottish university and college fees are not increasing. There have been concerns that English students could look to Scotland for cheaper tuition fees – and that a rush of students northwards would cut places available for Scottish students.

And it's been suggested that English students could face higher fees than their Scottish counterparts studying the same course at the same Scottish university or college. This could add another £700 per year to fees – up to around £1,900 – which would still be below the rate charged in England.

At present, English students at Scottish universities and colleges are means-tested for tuition fees by their own local education authority, in much the same way as if they were at an English university or college. But, as undergraduate degree courses in Scotland are often four years (rather than three in England), the extra year's tuition fee is paid for by the Student Awards Agency for Scotland. This arrangement could also disappear in the overhaul of fees next year.

32

Wales

Tuition fees

Students from Wales, like their English counterparts, are going to face a series of upheavals in funding in the next few years. Except that they're different upheavals. Because, while universities and colleges in England from 2006 will be able to charge up to £3,000 in so-called variable fees, this will not be the system for Wales.

The road for student funding is going to fork next year – with the English and Welsh systems going their separate ways. The national assembly in Wales has ruled out such variable fees until at least the end of the lifetime of the assembly, which will mean until 2007–08.

Instead, in 2006 Welsh students at Welsh universities and colleges will have a system of fixed tuition fees, with payment to be pushed back until after graduation. And it sounds as if it will be more like the current system in Scotland than either the present 'up-front' fees system in England or the variable fees to be introduced from next year.

Repayment of fees for Welsh higher education institutions will begin when graduates are working and earning more than £15,000 per year. The repayment rate will be 9 per cent of income above this level, with deductions taken from monthly salaries. But, for Welsh students at English universities and colleges, it will mean paying the higher rate of tuition fees that is being implemented next year, up to a maximum of £3,000 per year. These fees will no longer be paid up front, but will be repaid after graduation along with the student loans, and again after graduates have crossed the £15,000 earnings barrier.

There will be other aspects of the costs to parents that will remain similar to the English system.

Student loans

Student loans to cover living costs will be means-tested, with the amount of interest-free loan available dependent on the student's household income. If your parents are loaded, you'll get less of a loan than someone from a low-income family.

The current maximum loan, for students in London, is £5,175 per year – of which £3,880 is available to all students as a non-means-tested loan. This means that the parental contribution will be on a sliding scale between zero and £1,295, depending on their income. Parents are expected to begin contributions when their combined income is above £22,010.

Grants

As with students in England, from 2006 there will also be a means-tested non-repayable maintenance grant of up to £2,700.

In the longer term, no one really knows how this devolution in higher education will influence the decisions of young people in England, Wales, Scotland and Northern Ireland. Will this difference in fees deter Welsh students from attending English universities and colleges? Will it seem unfair that institutions over the border are charging fees that are so much higher? Or will students be indifferent to fees that will only be paid after university or college?

It's difficult to predict whether students will behave as higher education consumers, looking for a bargain, or whether they will consider quality above cost. And it also remains to be seen how this 'market' in variable fees will respond to any fluctuations in demand, as different higher education institutions, and different countries within the United Kingdom, compete for the same students.

33

Northern Ireland

Tuition fees

The current system of tuition fees and loans in Northern Ireland is, broadly speaking, the same as in England. But the complication is that future policy will be devolved, and that in turn is dependent on the outcome of Northern Ireland's political future. Without having a crystal ball available to determine the future of devolution in Northern Ireland, the present indications are that the higher tuition fees, which are to be introduced in England in 2006, will also apply to Northern Ireland.

While Scotland and Wales will be taking their own courses on student funding from 2006, the Northern Ireland Minister for Employment and Learning has aligned the Northern Irish system with the proposals for England. This will mean the end of up-front fees and the introduction of the repayments for fees after graduation and when former students are earning the equivalent of £15,000 per year. But the maximum level of tuition fees will rise sharply, from the current £1,175 per year to £3,000 per year.

In the meantime, if you are starting in 2005 you will have to pay the £1,175 annual tuition fee at the beginning of your course, unless you can claim a means-tested subsidy. You will continue under these arrangements throughout your university or college course.

Student loans

In terms of the repayment of student loans, this also follows the English system, with deductions taken directly each month from the salary of the former student, until the debt is cleared. When the £3,000 tuition fees are introduced in 2006, this will be added to the student loan debt, with the combined sum being repaid in monthly instalments once the £15,000 income threshold has been reached.

Republic of Ireland

If a Northern Irish student goes to a university or college in the Republic of Ireland, there is a charge of around 670 euros for exam fees and student services, which can be claimed back from the student's education and library board in Northern Ireland.

Teacher training

Another exception applies to subsidies for teacher training courses. In England, there can be financial incentives for students training to teach subjects where there is a shortage of teachers. But these so-called 'golden hellos' do not apply to courses in Northern Ireland. But, as with postgraduate teacher training (PGCE) courses in England, there is no tuition fee to be paid for this fourth year at university or college.

Part-time students

Part-time students in Northern Ireland will face tuition fees set by individual institutions, and can claim financial support from the Department for Employment Learning.

34

Overseas students

Overseas students, otherwise known as international students, are very popular with universities and colleges in this country, not least because they have to pay more than students from the United Kingdom (or the European Union, which counts as non-overseas).

Not just a bit more. Overseas students can be charged 10 times as much in tuition fees as home students. Even when these home students face higher fees in 2006, it will still be nowhere near as expensive as the cost for overseas students.

While students from the UK pay a tuition fee that is a contribution towards the costs, with a fixed upper limit, overseas students are charged whatever is the market rate. This brings the universities and colleges more cash – and there are some institutions which have talked about deliberately boosting the proportion of overseas students as a kind of subsidy for the loss-making home-grown students.

At the moment it is estimated that overseas students pay about £1.5 billion a year in fees. And some university and college courses are dependent on overseas students.

There is no fixed fee for overseas students, because they are individually set by universities and colleges and can vary between courses, with science courses usually costing more than the arts and humanities. But as a guide, for autumn 2005, a prestigious London university is quoting undergraduate fees of £10,500 per year for arts subjects and £13,750 for science and engineering subjects.

Elsewhere, in a 'new' university in southern England, annual fees for an undergraduate degree are between £7,200 and £8,540. At a leading university in northern England, overseas undergraduate students starting in autumn 2005 will be paying about £8,300 per year for an arts degree and £11,000 for a science degree. An MBA for business students charges fees of £17,500. Research-based postgraduate degrees will vary depending on the type of specialist course and subject – and universities will be able to advise about the charge.

All of the undergraduate fees are considerably more than the current £1,175 which UK students will be paying – and will still be much in excess of the £3,000 upper limit from 2006.

Fees are usually paid up front, but students who are self-supporting (which is to say, not sponsored by someone such as their government, another university or an employer) can sometimes pay in two instalments. It is also worth remembering that the figures quoted are only for the tuition fees and do not include the costs of rent, food and all the other everyday living expenses.

The London university mentioned above advises overseas students that they will need something like another £750 per month in living costs. Based on a nine-month year, this is going to mean another £6,750 to add to the budget. The university in northern England tells students to budget for about £6,600 for living costs for the academic year (and £8,700 for a full 12 months). Students will also have to pay for travel costs such as getting to the UK and flying home again for holidays.

Other charges

There are other charges which overseas students will have to take into account.

The cost of a visa for students has risen to £250 for an application by post and £500 for a faster, in-person service. These are still a little cheaper than a standard visa charge, but there were concerns from universities that this would be a disincentive for overseas students to come to the United Kingdom.

The British Council has forecast that there could be 870,000 overseas students in the United Kingdom by 2020, as higher education becomes an increasingly global market.

Part Four

Managing (without) money

There's nothing like the challenge of working at Costain

We have already created a high undersea cavern, as tall as three double-decker buses, for the Channel Tunnel; are responsible for the regeneration of St Pancras Station and St Martin-in-the-Fields, are currently building the Diamond Synchrotron Light Source – the largest scientific facility to be built in the UK for 30 years; and partnered the construction of the Jubilee Bridges across the Thames.

Now's your chance to find out if you could meet these kinds of challenges and begin an exciting and rewarding career.

1: How many graduates do you take a year and in which disciplines?
On average we employ between 50-60 graduates per year through out the business 50% of these will be Civil Engineers with Quantity Surveyors, Site Managers and Safety Health and Environmental graduates making up the remainder.

2: How do I apply?
Applicants are encouraged to apply through the Costain website and complete the online application form and attach their CV, although we do still accept paper applications.

3: What type of person are you looking for? (academic, personal, experience etc?)
We look for individuals who have a "can do" attitude and are capable of working as part of a team as well as on their own and are able to demonstrate this. Primarily we look to take on graduates who have or are completing a construction related degree, however we will consider non cognate degrees providing the graduate is able to demonstrate their desire to enter the construction industry. Experience of working within industry either through work experience, vacation work or Industrial placements does provide an advantage although this is not essential.

4: How do you evaluate the suitability of each applicant?
Graduates are initially assessed on the CV submitted, including presentation of information, degree course, previous academic results, evidence of team building and leadership, imitative and other information relating to extra curricular activities. If they meet the standards required they are invited to an

initial interview. If successful at passing the interview they will be invited to attend an assessment centre from which the final decision can be made.

5: How long is the graduate training scheme?

We offer a 3-year modular training scheme for graduates, which they tailor with an assigned supervisor to meet their needs. It includes the provision of up to 40 days off the job training and aims to help graduates become chartered in the minimum possible time.

6: What can I expect to do during graduate training?

Graduates can expect to be incorporated into one of our many countrywide project management teams. In most cases they will take on one of the traditional rolls open to a graduate or trainee in the construction industry. However in addition to the many site based construction roles we can offer some roles in the regional offices and Head Office.

Typical site based roles include: Site Engineer, Sub Contractor Management and Supervision, Safety and Environmental Management, Commercial Management of budgets and costs, document preparation, package Management, Coordination and Logistics of construction activities, Planning and Methodology.

Office based roles might include development of current initiatives such as Building Awareness (our work with schools and colleges), Supply Chain Management, Tendering, Estimating and Planning.

7: Salary & benefits?

Starting Package worth up to £22, 500 including car or car allowance, there is a biannual pay review for graduates, at the end of the training scheme salaries will be circa £25,000 + car or car allowance.

8: What are my prospects for career progression at the end of the scheme?

With a wide range of diversity and business opportunities within the company we do encourage individuals to develop and progress internally. We are a company that people join for the long term and we value the investment that individuals make, as part of our company culture.

9: Do I need to be geographically mobile? Where might I first be based?

Individuals do need to be geographically mobile as most of our roles are site based. We will always try to locate graduates within a commutable distance from their home location, however graduates first roles are likely to be project based and will depend on the requirements of the business.

Careers at Costain
beyond your expectations, not your grasp.

250 Bishopsgate, London – UK headquarters for a major european bank.

Slough Sewage Treatment Works for Thames Water.

Hungerford Bridge, one of London's landmarks, completed in 2002 by Costain in joint venture.

There's nothing like the challenge of working at Costain, one of the UK's leading engineering & construction companies, and our graduate intake is a vital part of our growth plans. The graduate programme is well established, constantly under development, tailored to the individual and designed to get you chartered in the minimum possible time.

We want to hear from graduates who are interested in becoming:

- **Quantity Surveyors** ● **Engineers (Civil, Mechanical & Electrical)** ● **Site Managers**
- **Safety & Environmental Advisors**

Candidates should have good communication skills and be team players. Graduates who have or are completing a construction related degree are preferred, however non cognate degrees will be considered providing the graduate is able to demonstrate a strong desire to enter the construction industry. Experience of working within industry either through work experience, vacation work or industrial placement is an advantage, but not essential.

If you are able to demonstrate a desire to successfully take on challenges that change the environment we live in for the better and you are committed to becoming professionally qualified, apply online at www.costain.com/careers or write to Jane Svendsen.

CONTACT COSTAIN: Jane Svendsen, Recruitment Coordinator,
Costain Limited, Costain House, Nicholsons Walk,
Maidenhead, Berkshire SL6 1LN.
EMAIL: careers@costain.com
www.costain.com/careers

Working towards equal opportunities.

COSTAIN

Where careers gather pace, not dust.

35

Budgeting

There's no point avoiding the fact that budgeting – the art of making ends meet and allocating your money carefully – sounds extremely dull. And even if you gave it a more upbeat sounding name, like 'prioritization assessment', it is still going to be the same porridge in a different bowl. But it's important, and is a good way of avoiding getting into a financial tangle – or, even worse, having to spend hours earning money to pay off interest charges that you didn't need to rack up in the first place.

Drawing up a budget means working out how much you have to spend and how much you are currently spending and then looking at where you should be targeting your meagre resources. It's the antidote to the kamikaze approach of spending three-quarters of the student loan in the first week and then not being able to afford a drink for the rest of term.

Spending

Draw up a list of what you spend each week or month and then allow for one-off expenditures that might be needed less often. What you're looking for is an honest breakdown of how you're spending your cash. And then it should be possible to introduce some forward planning in the financial department.

The way that the average student is currently spending money shows how uneven expenditure can be. Despite all the stereotypes, mobile phone spending is almost twice the spending on alcohol.

A budget is a good way of exposing these spending patterns and highlighting imbalances in finances. If you're having problems meeting repayments on credit cards or can't pay the rent, is it a good idea to buy expensive designer clothes?

No one can really answer these questions for someone else, but a budget is a way of giving yourself the information to make decisions. As a guide to the type of budget headings you might draw up, here are some typical expenses and forms of student income.

On the plus side there might be:

- student loan;
- parents' contribution;
- any bursaries or special grants;
- pay from part-time jobs.

Work out how much this represents as a weekly income.

Then you need to draw up a list, which is going to be depressingly longer, showing where the money is being spent. This might include:

- rent;
- food;
- clothes;
- fees;
- public transport;
- gas;
- electricity;
- water;
- mobile phone;
- credit card repayments;
- alcohol;
- nights out;
- taxis home;
- snacks;
- insurance;
- dvds/music;
- sports;
- hobbies;
- TV licence;
- internet;
- books;

- course equipment;
- stationery;
- train journey at end of term.

This is a rough guide to some typical expenses, but everyone will be able to add to this. If you're a cinema addict, maybe there should be another column for this. Or if you order take-aways every night, put this into your regular spending. People have very different interpretations of some of these headings. 'Food' could be a minimalist run through the supermarket essentials or it could be a lavish gourmet tour round the delicatessens. You could go out for an up-market meal for two and spend more than the cost of the weekly supermarket run.

There are other whole categories of cost that might apply. A growing number of students drive cars – and this means budgeting for insurance, tax, MOT, breakdown service, petrol and parking, not to mention any repairs it might need.

But you get the general picture. Work out how much – or, more to the point, how little – money is available for spending and then look at what the current commitments are costing.

If you are a new student, having to organize your budgets for the first time, this is a particularly useful exercise, as it focuses thoughts on expenses that previously were mysteriously covered by parents. When this assessment has depressed you enough, it could be time to work out how to claw back a little money for some reckless spending.

Students might not have as much spending power as people in work, but they do have opportunities to spend less money and live more cheaply. Whether it's cheaper beer in the student union or a student discount on public transport, there are opportunities for saving cash. Also, having more flexibility over time can make it easier to save. Train travel is cheaper when it's off-peak, cinema tickets can be cheaper at the beginning of the week.

Saving

There are often places to eat around universities and colleges which give a student discount, or there are some shops, such as music and DVD stores, which give discounts to students.

It's not only student discounts that can save money. If you take your money out of a cash machine that doesn't charge a fee it's going to save you the £1.50 or more that some other cash machines charge for exactly the same service.

Such money-saving tactics about finding bargains and avoiding rip-offs can be built up as you acquire local knowledge. But much of it is about common sense and planning. A designer coffee and a sandwich can cost a fiver – and if you treat yourself each week day, it's going to be £250 per term. That's probably enough to cover the whole term's electricity bill.

It is not about right or wrong, but more a question of making choices. It is also about taking responsibility for your money in a wider sense, and that can include considering other financial services, such as insurance.

Insurance

Students are notoriously likely to be burgled. They have plenty of consumer durables that attract burglars, and they're more likely than most to be living in rented, badly-secured properties. So it might be worth thinking about getting contents insurance, which protects against the loss of your possessions.

The cost of insurance is based on the perceived level of risk, and for contents insurance that usually means that the price is heavily influenced by the postcode. Put simply, if you live in a dodgy area with a high crime rate, the insurance is going to be more expensive.

The contents insurance might also offer a range of options depending on which items you want to cover. If you only want to cover your clothes, books and an old portable telly, it's going to be cheaper than if you want to include your state-of-the-art laptop and personal organizer.

There can also be options on whether you want the cover to extend to when you take your possessions outside, as well as when they're in your room. For a laptop, you have to think about what would happen if it were stolen when you took it to the library or if you left it on the bus. Parents might be able to extend their own contents insurance to provide some cover to their children away at university or college. This can sometimes come at no extra cost.

Students in halls of residence can sometimes have a collective insurance policy, negotiated by the university or college. But these might not cover high-value items such as laptops or bikes, and you might have to pay extra for them to be included.

Bank accounts

All of these ideas about looking after your money are about staying in control and making sure that you're not letting spending get out of hand. Many students say that they regularly check their accounts and make sure they know how much they have to spend and this is a sensible precaution.

Online banking can be a really useful help with this, as it gives you an instant picture of your finances. And there are services from some banks, such as texting your mobile to say when you're about to go overdrawn. And even though it won't make you any richer, keeping a close watch on your cash might stop you from taking a tumble into the financial twilight zone.

A profile of Oxford Brookes University

Oxford Brookes University is a leading, modern university with a national and international reputation for excellence in learning, teaching and research. Its multi-disciplinary academic and research portfolio is complemented with wider educational, social and cultural opportunities, creating a rich and lasting experience for its students of all ages and from every background.

The *Sunday Times University Guide 2004* described Oxford Brookes as 'indisputably the best modern university'. It achieves consistently high scores in the Government's teaching quality assessments, and is also one of the top 20 UK universities for graduate employability. With a strong and still growing reputation for postgraduate studies, just over a quarter of its students are on postgraduate courses. Research is also an expanding and important area, underpinning teaching at both undergraduate and postgraduate levels.

History

Oxford Brookes grew out of the Oxford City Technical School, founded in 1891 and incorporating the Oxford School of Art and School of Science. During the1950s, the institution became the College of Technology, and in 1970 it became Oxford Polytechnic. It received university status in 1992 and took the name Oxford Brookes University after John Henry Brookes, Principal of the Oxford City Technical School in 1928. Brookes' vision was to increase radically the access to education, a sentiment very much shared by the University today.

Statistics

The University has around 18,000 enrolled students and 2,600 staff. Its student body is made up of 71.7% undergraduates, 25.7% postgraduates, and 2.6% research.

International connections

For many decades, Oxford Brookes has been welcoming students from overseas. It values the academic and cultural contribution they make to the life of the university. More than 3,000 students from outside the UK are currently studying at the University in Oxford.

Oxford Brookes also has an expanding number of partnerships with fellow education providers around the world, where we share the benefit of our teaching and research skills.

Fees, Bursaries and Financial Support

The University provides comprehensive information on its web site:

http://www.brookes.ac.uk/services/finance/bursary.html

The Business School

The Business School is one of the largest Schools at Oxford Brookes University, with over 150 academic staff, more than 2,000 undergraduates and over 500 postgraduate and research students. It has built up an international reputation through its study programmes, research and consultancy. It offers single or combined honours programmes in a wide range of subject areas including: accounting; business and management; economics; finance; hospitality; human resources; information management; leisure; marketing; operations management; retail and tourism.

The Business School's courses in Business and Management and Economics were awarded top marks (24/24) following the most recent teaching quality assessments by the UK Governemnt's Quality assurance Agency (QAA). In 2005, the School were awarded a contract by to establish a Centre of Excellnce for Teaching and Learning.

Wherever possible the Business School programmes are designed to offer exemptions from the foundation examinations of Professional Associations such as CIMA -the Chartered Institute of Management Accountants or ACCA- the Association of Chartered Certified Accountants qualification. Exemptions depend on the combination of modules taken.

Student Testimonials

This link gives a good profile:

http://www.business.brookes.ac.uk/testimonials/undergraduate/
busmgmtstudentprofile.html

I worked at Marks and Spencer head office as a Product Developer in their Lingerie department during my placement year. Experiencing working for a major retailer and the day-to-day tasks of this role enabled me to decide if this was in fact the career that I wanted. My year at M&S definitely gave me an edge in the job market – I gained employment in the first position that I applied for upon graduating, in a hugely competitive job area.

The course, placement year option and facilities at Brookes helped me secure the job I wanted.

Victoria Simpson: BA (Hons) Retail and Business Management
Buyers Assistant, River Island

It was really helpful having support from the Oxford Brookes Placement team who worked hard to provide the first step when looking for jobs. I found the job working for BBC Worldwide on the Placements intranet site.

Gaining my degree at Brookes helped me get the job by giving me both practical transferable business skills and confidence. Studying a combined Marketing and Business degree has definitely aided my understanding of how the business operates and how the different departments and divisions work together to achieve the company's objectives.

Simon Bergenroth: BA Hons Business & Marketing Management
Marketing Assistant, BBC Worldwide

36

Student debt

For students, managing money is really about trying to manage without money. And the threat of debt is one of the reasons that will make some young people think twice about going to college or university. In a major annual survey of student attitudes, there were two leading contenders for the 'worst aspect' of student life: 'Having little money' and 'Being in debt'. Following up in third place was 'No regular income'.

Debt has become part of the culture. Students leave university or college owing a mountain of money. And every year the mountain seems to get higher, as surveys record the dizzying upward climb of the debt totals. And the figures get so high that it's hard to get a grip on what people are really likely to owe when they leave university or college. £10,000? £20,000? Do I hear any advance on £30,000?

These are for that mythical beast, the 'average' student. There are other stories of extreme cases, where students have been playing frisbee with their credit cards and run up debts of £50,000 and £60,000. And hard-headed debt counsellors will tell you that they have met terrifying cases of students, with huge debts, who have been given loans without any obvious way of paying any of it back.

But these are the extremes. What we want to know are the prospects for most ordinary students who don't have hyperactive spending habits.

All the evidence suggests that debt has been rising for students. The current estimates from bank surveys, including Barclays and NatWest, put average graduate debt at around £12,000. The Unite/Mori annual survey gives a lower figure of just below £10,000.

But, either way, it's a daunting figure before you've even started work. This is going to rise even higher, because the threefold increase in tuition fees in 2006 will be pushed onto the debt to be paid back after graduation.

A survey from the National Institute of Economic and Social Research says that higher fees will cause a 54 per cent increase in student debt. And, taking the current estimates of student debt, that would mean future average debt of about £15,000 to £18,000. This forecast is more conservative than bank projections, which have included claims that graduate debt will rise to £33,000.

But before hitting the panic buttons, what is really meant by student debt? And is it possible to avoid such a high amount of borrowing?

What is student debt?

That might sound like a dumb question. But it's worth breaking down the headline figures and trying to understand what it really means to the individual.

The figures for student debt are also known as 'graduate debt', because they are based on how much debt a student has built up by the time they leave higher education. Students need money to keep them housed, fed and entertained when they're at university or college, so they borrow the money to make this possible.

The biggest loans will come from the Student Loans Company – and students outside London can borrow up to £4,195 per year. Over three years, this means that students will owe the Student Loans Company more than £12,000. That's a great deal of money, but it's not like a commercial debt, because it's an interest-free advance which is repaid once the student is in regular employment.

The money does have to be paid back, but it isn't nearly as punitive as a young person owing a similar amount on an interest-charging credit card. (The real problem for students is that they can end up with the credit card debt as well as the student loan.) It's worth separating the elements of the debt. If the only money that is owed by a student is to the Student Loans Company, it's much less depressing than the headline figure suggests.

If someone offered a £12,000 car loan which was permanently interest free, only had to be paid back when your salary was high enough, perhaps years after you'd bought the car, we would all assume there was a catch in the small print.

Bear in mind also that these figures of £10,000 to £12,000 graduate debt are averages. If the lower figure is correct, it suggests that some students are not even using their full loan. Or, more likely, they are working in part-time jobs to reduce their borrowing. It also means that there are many students out there who are borrowing much more than these averages, who have had to supplement the loan with borrowing from banks, credit cards and other lenders.

Again, still looking at the official student loans, you can draw very different impressions from the same information. The total amount owed by students to the Student Loans Company is an eye-watering £14.6 billion, which sounds like every student in the land must be weighed down with appalling debts. But the same annual figures show that a quarter of debts paid back to the Student Loans Company were early payments by people able and willing to pay off their loans earlier than was required.

Anyone who has been to university or college recently will also tell you that there is no such thing as an 'average' student. While some students from low and middle-income families are toiling away on a threadbare loan, there are other richer students who have had the run of Daddy's credit card, and for whom debt is always going to be someone else's problem.

All of these students will appear to have 'debts', but the same debt can have a very different meaning to students from different backgrounds. It is often trotted out that working-class students are traditionally more 'debt averse' – but that could be for the very good reason that no one else is going to help them pay it back.

It's important to distinguish between the types of debt that are rolled together into the student debt totals. There's no such thing as a good debt. But there are degrees of badness. And the official student loans are certainly at the least bad end of the scale, as they don't charge interest, there is no time pressure for repayment, and payments are not imposed when someone is broke and out of work. If you reach the end of your course as a student and only owe money on your student loans, you won't have done too badly.

Reducing debt

Meanwhile, back in the real world, students will be saying that there's no way that they can get by on just the student loan. How would you expect to live on £5,175 in London for a year? And that's assuming that any parental contribution is paid in full.

If when you graduate your only debts are to the Student Loans Company, then students will say it means one of three things: you've either been subsidized heavily by your well-off family, you've worked every night in a pizza restaurant or you've hit the jackpot with bursaries and scholarships.

Because most students will struggle to get by on their student loan, and there are temptations all around to borrow more, the money owed to the Student Loans Company is only part of a more complicated pattern of debt. Credit cards, overdrafts and personal loans will all be dangled in front of students.

Even though it might not be realistic to say that students shouldn't borrow beyond the student loan, there is certainly plenty to be gained from a damage limitation exercise. Borrowing more efficiently will mean real savings, and if you're a cash-strapped student, why pay extra to the banks?

To begin with, think of a loan not as a means of buying something you really want, but as a commodity, like a box of soap powder on the supermarket shelves. And, like anything else in the supermarket, it has a price tag. You might want something, but how much do you want to pay for it?

When you take out a loan, the price tag is the interest rate, charges and length of repayment. And different loans have different prices.

If the bank will give you an interest-free overdraft while you're at university or college, that's going to be a real cash saving against running up the same amount of debt on an expensive store card. You'll have had the same amount of extra money to spend, but the price tag will be entirely different.

There can be huge differences in the interest rates. Store cards, often plugged by sales staff at the cash tills in clothes shops, can have interest rates that are approaching a vertigo-inducing 30 per cent APR. If you don't clear the balance, this is going to become very expensive very quickly. Store cards, with a few honourable exceptions, are usually at the expensive end of the scale. But there are big differences between credit cards.

Apart from the zero per cent introductory offers, credit cards can vary widely in interest charges. These change from week to week, so there is no point recommending a specific card now. But there is plenty of free information available showing the current list of the most competitive credit cards, in the personal finance section of newspapers or else on the internet. As a starting point, www.money facts.co.uk will have details of the current crop of cards with the lowest interest rates.

Check out the deals available – and examine whether you can shift any credit card balances to a card with a lower interest rate or a zero per cent offer. This will only take a few phone calls, but the savings will be worth it.

Make sure you understand what you're being offered. A bank might give you an interest-free overdraft, but that will only be up to an agreed limit. If your overdraft goes above this level, this becomes an 'unauthorized overdraft', and the interest charges can go through the roof. If this happens, it can be cheaper to arrange a loan from the bank, with structured repayments, than to run up a load of interest charges on the overdraft.

But it's even better to avoid getting into this kind of problem in the first place.

Although it is irritatingly easy to be wise from the sidelines, the problem with managing debt on a low income is that repayments and interest charges soon begin to eat into the small amount of spending money you have available. And the temptation then is to get a little more breathing space by borrowing more money – and jumping into debt is much quicker and easier than the slow crawl back out of debt.

Every pound not borrowed means less interest to pay back, so any debt avoided by getting a job, cutting spending or borrowing more intelligently can have a long-term, cumulative benefit.

What if debt becomes a serious problem?

Students spend most of their time at university or college in debt. But there are more acute versions of this problem, and when interest charges start to spiral like the world's worst taxi meter and your finances are spinning out of control, it's time to get help.

You won't be alone, because about one in 20 students falls into the category of getting into serious financial difficulties. And the first thing to recognize is that there is no point hiding away and hoping it will disappear. In fact, one of the classic signs of a debt problem is when you start dreading the post.

But don't ignore the letters from lenders or think that you can borrow your way out of a corner. If it is becoming impossible to meet the repayments, ask for help at the student union, the welfare office, the bank or go directly to debt advisers, such as the Consumer Credit Counselling Service, which has its own confidential student helpline, on 0800 328 1813.

There is also likely to be a local office of Citizens Advice, where you can go to get free advice. Details will be available from student union welfare officers, or look it up on the internet.

When you are facing financial problems, it's extremely stressful and hard to make decisions, and it's better to get the perspective of someone who can offer more objective advice and who can contact lenders on your behalf.

The Consumer Credit Counselling Service will give individualized advice, but it also has a list of suggestions to help students who are in financial difficulties:

1. Make sure that you're receiving the entire student loan to which you're entitled.
2. If you're working, make sure that you're paying the right tax. The first £4,615 can be earned without being taxed.
3. Budget to plan expenditure and to avoid over-spending.
4. Look for a bank account with better deals for students.
5. Look to see if there are any bursaries to which you could apply for extra support.
6. Look for a credit card with a better interest rate.
7. Travel off-peak and make savings on fares.

The debt advisers can negotiate repayment deals with creditors, and help defuse the immediate pressure for money, and they can give advice on how to prioritize spending.

It's important to resolve the underlying problems which have caused the over-spending, and advisers can draw up a detailed budget showing how much someone can afford to spend each week, without having to pile up the debts on the credit card. Debt counsellors won't have a magic wand, and they won't be able to get lenders to write off the debt, but they will be able to suggest a practical way out of the problem.

Students have a particularly unusual type of income, where it comes in large blocks at the beginning of term. And if this loan payment gets blown too early, or there are unexpected expenses, it can soon mean that students are borrowing more than they intended, with no regular monthly salary to make repayments.

Once a couple of repayments are missed, anyone who has been in debt will tell you how quickly it can turn into financial quicksand. Even if people are working extra shifts and trying to make ends meet, the debt can feel like a big black hole swallowing everything. And students, away from home and suddenly facing a doormat covered in threatening letters, can feel very intimidated and isolated by debt problems. So don't hesitate to get help sooner rather than later.

37

Banks love students

Banks love students. It might not feel like it, but you'll never be as much in demand as when you're looking for a bank account in which to lodge your student loan. This is because the banks know that once a customer opens an account he or she is likely to stay with that bank for many years. The cliché that's usually trotted out about this is that people are more likely to get divorced than leave their bank.

So, when you're looking for a bank account, remember it's a buyer's market. The banks assume that today's students will be tomorrow's higher earners, so they're ready to offer inducements to attract you.

But don't be suckered into choosing a bank for the sake of twenty quid's worth of CD vouchers or a few free cinema tickets. These marketing ploys can be quite imaginative, offering discounts on curries and computer games or a free driving lesson. Don't be distracted, because the amount they are worth is going to be less than something like an interest-free overdraft for three years. So look carefully at the long-term value of the bank's services.

The offers made by banks change every year, so don't listen to people saying that a particular bank is always the best or worst for students. This is a competitive market and banks will be launching different student accounts each year to try to stay ahead of their rivals. Check out what they're offering against what you'll need.

You can either check out the individual bank offers, either by a trip along the high street to pick up leaflets, or else look on bank websites, where there will be a section for students. You can always tell these student banking areas on corporate websites, because they're usually painfully trying to be funky, with lots of upbeat colours and graphics, which can look a bit too much like the boring geography teacher trying to get hip with the kids.

Even quicker than going to individual bank websites, there are useful one-stop-shop sites that have lists of the current student offers from banks. An established online source for this is www.money facts.co.uk, which has a list of the services currently available for student accounts from all the major banks. Once you've got this kind of overview of what's available, think about what's going to be useful.

First of all, make sure that a bank is going to be a practical proposition for where you're going to be a student. Not all banks will have a branch on or near your campus, so check out the availability of branches and cash machines. If you need advice or are heading for current account meltdown, it can be very useful to have a branch where you can talk face-to-face with bank staff who understand student finances.

Student accommodation now often comes with internet access, and online banking is a useful way of keeping up to date with how much money you have left. So check if any prospective bank can give you online banking. If not, shop around to see where it is available.

Putting aside the usually pretty dismal bribes on offer from banks, the biggest selling points will be how much low-cost support they can offer. It's no secret that when you're a student you're often going to have an empty bank account, which will mean that an interest-free overdraft is very important if you're going to avoid running up a debt on credit cards.

The amount of interest-free overdraft available, at the time of writing, varies between £1,000 and £2,000 – and many banks increase the overdrafts available to students during their time at university or college. This is a valuable perk, as it means not paying interest on other kinds of borrowing.

But be warned – this is still a loan and not a gift, and students will have to start paying off this debt once they graduate, or else face interest charges. Many banks also have graduate deals, which soften the blow of the transition from student accounts.

Beyond the interest-free overdraft, there can be 'authorized' overdrafts, where banks will charge interest for borrowing up to an agreed limit. Compare how much interest is charged and how much money they will lend. At present, authorized interest rates on student accounts can be between 6 and 9 per cent APR.

If you go beyond this limit you enter the shark-infested waters of the 'unauthorized overdraft', which is where you start spending money that the bank hasn't offered to lend you. This is a bad idea and the interest penalties are going to shred your money. Interest charges for unauthorized overdrafts are currently between 13 and 31 per cent APR. There can also be separate one-off charges for going into this unauthorized overdraft zone.

Credit cards

If you want a credit card, make sure that the bank will give them to students, and then look at the type of limits available. At present, these range between £250 and £600, but these limits will be negotiable depending on individual circumstances.

Banks will also lend money to students, beyond the overdraft, to supplement student loans. And these can be at rates that are more competitive than those available for non-students. Last year's students were offered almost £5,000 in a loan by a bank, with repayments at 1 per cent above the base rate. Again, this would have been a better option than running up debts on store cards or most commercial loan rates.

But as with all offers of easy borrowing, the comfort factor can be dangerously seductive, and students, who have little income for three years, can quickly heap up the debts and create a real problem for themselves when the borrowing has to be paid back. Banks will provide overdrafts, loans and credit cards, but they're going to have to be paid back when students are already having to start paying off their student loans.

For the eternal optimists, it's also worth checking out how much interest the banks will pay you when you're in credit. A lump sum like a loan cheque can briefly generate some interest. It's not exactly going to keep you in luxury, but it might be enough to buy you a drink to go with the discount curry.

Golden Opportunities with the ACA qualification

With so many factors to consider when planning your university career and choices after your degree, it's sometimes hard to make sense of the options available to you. Key aspects to consider in that all important education and career decision making process include, what degree is right for me? What job will provide the right training? Will there be a high salary to help pay debts off as quickly as possible after I graduate? Future job security? Variety? Opportunities to travel? Prestige? But is there the career out there that can really match all these requirements, whilst giving you the financial stability you are looking for?

How about Chartered Accountancy?

There are many misconceptions and stereotypes of accountants, but the fact is, there are few better routes to a career at the heart of business than the ACA qualification from the Institute of Chartered Accountants in England & Wales (ICAEW), or a better route to a stable and often well paid career.

What is Chartered Accountancy?

Chartered Accountants are first and foremost, business advisers, underpinning the smooth running of just about any organisation. Chartered Accountants concentrate efforts on deciding where organisations are heading and how best to get there.

Choice and variety are the key elements of the career. Those who decide to join the profession work and train alongside like-minded people of a similar age, testing their skills to the limit and experiencing a whole range of challenging projects.

There are training opportunities in firms of Chartered Accountants (Public Practice) the Public Sector and Commerce. Once qualified, ACAs work in all sectors of business in the UK and overseas.

The ACA qualification

The ICAEW which offers the ACA, is the largest professional body in Europe with some 126,000 members. We have over 3000 students entering training every year after graduating. By training for the ACA, you gain a professional qualification whilst earning a very competitive salary which increases as you pass your exams, and generally by the time you qualify your salary will double, not a bad prospect when weighing up the cost of going to university and the impact your university study may then have on your future bank balance!

The Training

The ACA qualification is unique in that students are required to complete a 3 year training contract within one of the ICAEWs 2200 authorised training offices. An authorised employer is an employer that has been checked by the ICAEW to ensure they can provide all the support and work experience needed to qualify.

There are two stages to ACA training, the Professional Stage which provides an understanding of the concepts and principles of accounting. Second is the Advanced Stage, during which students apply the theoretical knowledge to real business issues in preparation for a final assessment.

Graduate entry to Chartered Accountancy

The majority of ACA trainees start their training contract after completing a degree. ACA trainees enter the profession from a variety of degree disciplines. It's the results that count more than the type of degree, you will generally need a 2:1 or 1st class honours, together with good A level results to secure a training contract. A level Maths or a Finance related degree are not essential, but you will need to be able to demonstrate key skills essential to progressing your career, such as communication and presentation skills, teamwork and commercial awareness.

Next Steps

Study a degree you are going to enjoy and that interests you! Take note of careers events and opportunities that exist during your time at university to find out more about your options, plan early and think about what you want to do after your degree, if a career with variety, opportunity and a good salary is what you want then apply for an ACA Training Contract. If you take on part time work whilst you are studying, think about the skills you are learning that you can then apply to a future career, all this will help you to stand out from the crowd!

To find out more about the ACA qualification, career prospects and training vacancies, go to **www.icaew.co.uk/careers** email **careers@icaew.co.uk** or call our student support helpline **01908 248040**.

Where are all the Golden opportunities?

Appendix: Contacts, information and advice

Universities and Colleges Admissions Service (UCAS)
Rosehill
New Barn Lane
Cheltenham
Gloucestershire GL52 3LZ
Tel: 01242 222444
Website: www.ucas.com

Department for Education and Skills (DfES)
Tel: 0800 731 9133
Website:
www.dfes.gov.uk/studentsupport

Another useful DEFS website with advice, information and application forms to download is:
www.studentfinancedirect.co.uk

A list of local education authority contacts can be found at:
www.dfes.gov.uk/studentsupport/students/lea_lea_contact_det.shtml

Hotcourses Ltd
150–152 King Street
London W6 0QU
Tel: 020 8600 5300
Website: www.studentmoney.org

Student Awards Agency for Scotland
Gyleview House
3 Redheughs Rigg
South Gyle
Edinburgh EH12 9HH
Tel: 0131 476 8212
Website: www.student-support-saas.gov.uk

Welsh Assembly Government
Higher Education Division 2
3rd Floor
Cathays Park
Cardiff CF10 3NQ
Tel: 02920 825831
Website: www.learning.wales.gov.uk

Department for Employment and Learning (DELNI)
Adelaide House
39/49 Adelaide Street
Belfast
BT2 8FD
Tel: 02890 257777
Website: www.delni.gov.uk

Student Loans Company
100 Bothwell Street
Glasgow G2 7JD
Tel: 0800 405 010
Website: www.slc.co.uk

National Union of Students
Nelson Mandela House
461 Holloway Road
London N7 6LJ
Tel: 020 7272 8900
Website: www.nusonline.co.uk

NUS Scotland
29 Forth Street
Edinburgh EH1 3LE
Tel: 0131 556 6598
Website: www.nusonline.co.uk/scotland

National Union of Students/Union of Students in Ireland
29 Bedford Street
Belfast BT2 7EJ
Tel: 02890 244641
Website: www.nistudents.org

Aim Higher university information
Website: www.aimhigher.ac.uk

European Union students
The European Team
Department for Education and Skills
2F Area B
Mowden Hall
Staindrop Road
Darlington
Co Durham DL3 9BG
Tel: 01325 391199
Website:
www.dfes.gov.uk/studentsupport/eustudents/index.shtml

Teacher Training Agency
Portland House
Stag Place
London SW1E 5TT
Tel: 020 7925 3700
Website: www.tta.gov.uk

Healthcare students

The leaflet Financial Help for Health Care Students is available free from:
Department of Health Publications
PO Box 777
London SE1 6XH

NHS Careers Helpline
Tel: 0845 606 0655

NHS Students Grants Unit
22 Plymouth Road
Blackpool FY3 7JS
Tel: 01253 655655

NHS Wales Student Awards Unit
2nd Floor
Golate House
101 St Mary Street
Cardiff CF10 1DX
Tel: 02920 261495

The Students Awards Agency for Scotland
3 Redheughs Rigg
South Gyle
Edinburgh EH12 9HH
Tel: 0131 476 8212

The Department of Higher and Further Education Training and Employment
Student Support Branch
4th Floor Adelaide House
39–49 Adelaide Street
Belfast BT2 8FD

Social work students

Bursary schemes are managed by the General Social Care Council, details from:
GSCC Bursaries
General Social Care Council
Bursaries Office
Goldings House
2 Hay's Lane
London SE1 2HB
Website:
www.gscc.org.uk/bursaries.htm

Care Council for Wales
Student Funding Team
7th Floor
Southgate House
Wood Street
Cardiff CF10 1EW

Postgraduate funding

Arts and Humanities Research Council
Tel: 0117 987 6543
Website: www.ahrb.ac.uk

Biotechnology and Biological Sciences Research Council
Tel: 01793 413200
Website: www.bbsrc.ac.uk

Engineering and Physical Sciences Research Council
Tel: 01793 444100
Website: www.epsrc.ac.uk

Economic and Social Research Council
Tel: 01793 413000
Website: www.esrc.ac.uk

Medical Research Council
Tel: 020 7636 5422
Website: www.mrc.ac.uk

Natural Environment Research Council
Tel: 01793 411500
Website: www.nerc.ac.uk

Particle Physics and Astronomy Research Council
Tel: 01793 442000
Website: www.pparc.ac.uk

Support and money advice

Citizens Advice
Website: www.citizensadvice.org.uk
Check in phone book for local office

Consumer Credit Counselling Service
Tel: 0800 138 1111
Website: www.cccs.co.uk

National Debtline
Tel: 0808 808 4000
Website: www.nationaldebtline.co.uk

Index

Index of advertisers

Financing your future

A further period of academic study or vocational training can really make a graduate job applicant stand out from the crowd. The only problem is that when you're leaving university with a student loan as well as degree, finding the finance for another course can seem pretty daunting.

That's where a Career Development Loan can help. Designed as the result of a government initiative, Career Development Loans help to make sure that a lack of money doesn't get in the way of vocational training. The Department for Education and Skills will pay the interest on the loan while you are studying and for up to one month afterwards. You can then spread the repayments over the following 1 to 5 years.

You can apply for a Career Development Loan from The Co-operative Bank for any amount between £300 and £8,000, knowing that you will not have to repay a penny whilst you study – or for up to one month after you have completed your course. The rate of interest is fixed as soon as your loan is agreed.

For example, say you are applying for a 12 month course which starts on 1 October 2005. You don't pay anything for 13 months as the government pays the interest for you. After that, you can pay off your loan over the agreed period of 1 to 5 years.

To find out more about a Career Development Loan from The Co-operative Bank, simply phone **08457 212 212**, call into your local branch or visit our website on **www.co-operativebank.co.uk**